EYEWITNESS TRAVEL
PHRASE BOOK
MANDARIN
CHINESE

REVISED EDITION

DK LONDON

Senior Editor Christine Stroyan
Senior Art Editors Anna Hall, Amy Child
Art Director Karen Self
Associate Publisher Liz Wheeler
Publishing Director Jonathan Metcalf
Proofreading Andiamo! Language Services Limited
Senior Pre-Producer Andy Hilliard
Senior Producers Gary Batchelor, Anna Vallarino

DK DELHI

Assistant Editor Sugandha Agarwal
Assistant Art Editors
Anukriti Arora, Rohit Bhardwaj,
Devika Khosla, Shubham Rastogi
Art Editor Mohd. Zishan
Senior Art Editor Chhaya Sajwan
Managing Editor Soma B. Chowdhury
Senior Managing Art Editor
Arunesh Talapatra

Production Manager Pankaj Sharma
Preproduction Managers
Sunil Sharma, Balwant Singh
Senior DTP Designers
Tarun Sharma, Vishal Bhatia,
Neeraj Bhatia, Ajay Verma

First American edition 2008
This revised edition published in 2017 by
DK Publishing,
345 Hudson Street, New York, New York 10014

Copyright © 2008, 2017 Dorling Kindersley Limited
DK, a Division of Penguin Random House LLC
17 18 19 20 10 9 8 7 6 5 4 3 2 1
001–300200–Jun/2017

A catalog record for this book is available from the Library of Congress.
ISBN: 978-1-4654-6266-4

Printed and bound in China

A WORLD OF IDEAS:
SEE ALL THERE IS TO KNOW
www.dk.com

CONTENTS

INTRODUCTION

This book provides all the key words and phrases you are likely to need in everyday situations. It is grouped into themes, and key phrases are broken down into short sections to help you build a wide variety of sentences. A lot of the vocabulary is illustrated to make it easy to remember, and "You may hear" boxes feature questions that you are likely to hear. At the back of the book there is a menu guide, listing about 300 food terms, and a 3,500-word dictionary. Numbers are printed on the last page of the book for quick reference.

NOUNS

In Chinese, the plural of nouns is normally the same as the singular. There is also no direct equivalent of the English "a/an" or "the."

ADJECTIVES

Chinese adjectives may have different endings depending on how they are used, and are also very often preceded by **hen** ("very").

VERBS

Verbs have no tenses and do not generally change according to who or what the subject is, but there are some characters that can be added in order to indicate a particular mood or time:

to come	lái
is coming	lái le
isn't coming	bù lái le
came	lái guò
didn't come	méi lái guò
please come!	lái ba!

PRONUNCIATION GUIDE

The Chinese phrases in this book are given in Mandarin Chinese, the main language of the People's Republic of China (PRC). Below each Chinese word or phrase, you will find a pronunciation guide in italics. The pronunciation is written in Pinyin, the official Romanization system.

Simple vowels

a	"a" in "father" (never like "cat")
e	rhymes roughly with the "ir" in "bird" at the end of a syllable. Otherwise it can sound more like the "e" in "men," depending on the speaker.
i	"i" in "machine." Written "yi" at the beginning of a syllable.
o	rhymes with "law"
u	rhymes with "loop." Written "wu" at the beginning of a syllable. Exceptions: "ju," "qu," "xu," and "yu" are pronounced as "ü." The "y" of "yu" is not pronounced.
ü	like German ü or French "u." Protrude the lips as if saying "boo" but actually say "ee."

Vowel combinations

ai	rhymes with "why"
ao	rhymes roughly with "cow"
ei	rhymes with "cake"
ia	rhymes with "car." Written "ya" at the beginning of a syllable.
ie	as in "yes." Written "ye" at the beginning of a syllable.
ou	"go," "toe"
ua	"w" followed by Pinyin "a." Written "wa" at the beginning of a syllable.
uai	"w" followed by Pinyin "ai." Written "wai" at the beginning of a syllable.
ue / üe	Pinyin "ü" followed by "e" as in "bet." Written "yue" at the beginning of a syllable.
uo	Pinyin "u" followed by Pinyin "o." Written "wo" at the beginning of a syllable.

Most consonants are quite similar to their English equivalents.
The following are the difficult ones:

j	similar to English "j." Note that a following "u" becomes "ü."
q	like "ch" in "choke." Note that a following "u" becomes "ü."
x	pronounced as "hs." Note that a following "u" becomes "ü"
z	pronounced as "dz"—"bad zone"
c	pronounced as "ts"—"its"

FREE EYEWITNESS TRAVEL
PHRASE BOOK AUDIO APP

The audio app that accompanies this phrase book contains nearly
1,000 essential Chinese words and phrases, spoken by native speakers,
for use when traveling or when preparing for your trip.

HOW TO USE THE AUDIO APP

- Download the free app on your smartphone or tablet from the
  App Store or Google Play.
- Open the app and scan or key in the barcode on the back of your
  Eyewitness Phrase Book to add the book to your Library.
- Download the audio files for your language.
- The 🎧 symbol in the book indicates that there is audio for that
  section. Enter the page number from the book into the search field
  in the app to bring up the list of words and phrases for that page or
  section. You can then scroll up and down through the list to find the
  word or phrase you want.
- Tap a word or phrase to hear it.
- Swipe left or right to view the previous or next page.
- Add phrases you will use often to your Favorites.

3 0053 01262 5607

ESSENTIALS

In this section, you will find the essential words and useful phrases that you will need for basic everyday talk and situations in China. Traditionally, when Chinese people greet each other, they cup one hand inside the other, in front of the chest, and they may nod or bow slightly. However, due to increasing Western influence, they may shake hands with you now instead, especially if you are traveling to China on business.

GREETINGS

Hello
你好
nǐhǎo

Good morning
早上好
zǎoshànghǎo

Good evening
晚上好
wǎnshànghǎo

Good night
晚安
wǎn'ān

Goodbye
再见
zàijiàn

How are you?
你好吗?
nǐhǎoma

Fine, thanks
我很好,谢谢
wǒhěnhǎo, xièxie

You're welcome
不用谢
búyòngxiè

My name is...
我叫...
wǒjiào

What's your name?
你叫什么名字?
nǐ jiào shénme míngzì

What's his/her name?
他/她叫什么名字?
tā/tā jiào shénme míngzì

This is...
这是...
zhèshì

Pleased to meet you
很高兴认识你
hěngāoxìng rènshi nǐ

See you soon
回见
huíjiàn

See you tomorrow
明天见
míngtiānjiàn

ESSENTIALS

SMALL TALK

Yes/no	是/不是 *shì/búshì*
Please	请 *qǐng*
Thank you (very much)	（非常）谢谢你 *(fēicháng) xièxienǐ*
You're welcome	不用谢 *búyòngxiè*
OK/fine	可以/好的 *kěyǐ / hǎode*
Pardon?	请再说一遍? *qǐng zài shuō yībiàn*
Excuse me	劳驾 *láojià*
Sorry	对不起 *duìbuqǐ*
I don't know	不知道 *bùzhīdào*
I don't understand	我不明白 *wǒ bù míngbai*
Could you repeat that?	你能重复一遍么? *nǐ néng chóngfù yībiàn ma*
I don't speak Chinese	我不会说中文 *wǒ búhuì shuō zhōngwén*
Do you speak English?	你会说英文么? *nǐ huì shuō yīngwén ma*
What is the Chinese for...	中文...怎么说 *zhōngwén ...zěnme shuō*
What's that called?	那叫什么? *nà jiào shénme*
Can you tell me...	你能告诉我...吗 *nǐ néng gàosù wǒ...ma*

TALKING ABOUT YOURSELF

I'm from...	我来自... *wǒ láizì*
I'm...	我是... *wǒshì*
...American	...美国人 *měiguó rén*
...English	...英国人 *yīngguó rén*
...Canadian	...加拿大人 *jiānádà rén*
...Australian	...澳大利亚人 *àodàlìyà rén*
...single	...单身 *dānshēn*
...married	...已婚 *yǐhūn*
...divorced	... 离婚了 *líhūnle*
I am...years old	我...岁 *wǒ ...suì*
I have...	我有... *wǒyǒu*
...brothers/sisters	...兄弟/姐妹 *xiōngdì /jiěmèi*
...a son/daughter	...儿子/女儿 *érzi/nǚér*
Where are you from?	你来自哪里? *nǐ láizì nǎlǐ*
Are you married?	你结婚了么? *nǐ jiéhūnle ma*
Do you have children?	你有孩子么? *nǐ yǒu háizi ma*

SOCIALIZING

Do you live here?
你住这儿吗？
nǐ zhù zhèr ma

Where do you live?
你住哪儿？
nǐ zhù nǎr

I am here...
我在这儿...
wǒ zài zhèr

...on vacation
...度假
dùjià

...on business
...出差
chūchāi

I'm a student
我是学生
wǒ shì xuésheng

I work in...
我在...工作
wǒ zài ...gōngzuò

I am retired
我退休了
wǒ tuìxiūle

Can I have...
可以给我...
kěyǐ gěiwǒ

...your telephone number?
...你的电话号码吗？
nǐde diànhuà hàomǎ ma

...your email address?
...你的电子邮件吗？
nǐde diànzǐyóujiàn ma

It doesn't matter
没关系
méiguānxi

Cheers!
谢了！
xièle

Are you alright?
你没事吧？
nǐ méishì ba

Do you mind if I smoke?
你介意我抽烟么？
nǐ jièyì wǒ chōuyān ma

I'm OK
我很好
wǒ hěnhǎo

LIKES AND DISLIKES

I like/love...

我喜欢/爱...
wǒ xǐhuan /ài

I don't like...

我不喜欢...
wǒ bùxǐhuan

I hate...

我讨厌...
wǒ tǎoyàn

I rather/really like...

我十分/很喜欢...
wǒ shífēn /hěn xǐhuan

Don't you like it?

你喜欢这个吗?
nǐ xǐhuan zhège ma

I would like...

我想要...
wǒ xiǎngyào

I'd like this one/that one

我想要这个/那个
wǒ xiǎngyào zhège /nàge

My favorite is...

我最喜欢...
wǒ zuì xǐhuan

I prefer...

我更喜欢...
wǒ gèng xǐhuan

It's delicious

好吃
hǎochī

What would you like
to do?

你想做什么?
nǐ xiǎng zuò shénme

I don't mind

我无所谓
wǒ wúsuǒwèi

Do you like...?

你喜欢...吗?
nǐxǐhuan ...ma

YOU MAY HEAR...

你做什么的　　你在休假么
nǐ zuò shénme de　*nǐ zàixiūjià ma*
What do you do?　**Are you on vacation?**

DAYS OF THE WEEK 🎧

What day is it today?	今天星期几? *jīntiān xīngqījǐ*	Friday	星期五 *xīngqīwǔ*
Sunday	星期天 *xīngqītiān*	Saturday	星期六 *xīngqīliù*
Monday	星期一 *xīngqīyī*	today	今天 *jīntiān*
Tuesday	星期二 *xīngqīèr*	tomorrow	明天 *míngtiān*
Wednesday	星期三 *xīngqīsān*	yesterday	昨天 *zuótiān*
Thursday	星期四 *xīngqīsì*	in...days	...天之内 *tiānzhīnèi*

THE SEASONS 🎧

春天
chūntiān
spring

夏天
xiàtiān
summer

MONTHS

January	一月 *yīyuè*	July	七月 *qīyuè*
February	二月 *èryuè*	August	八月 *bāyuè*
March	三月 *sānyuè*	September	九月 *jiǔyuè*
April	四月 *sìyuè*	October	十月 *shíyuè*
May	五月 *wǔyuè*	November	十一月 *shíyīyuè*
June	六月 *liùyuè*	December	十二月 *shí'èryuè*

秋天
qiūtiān
fall

冬天
dōngtiān tiān
winter

ESSENTIALS

TELLING THE TIME 🎧

What time is it?	现在几点？ *xiànzài jǐdiǎn*
It's nine o'clock	九点 *jiǔdiǎn*
...in the morning	...上午 *shàngwǔ*
...in the afternoon	...下午 *xiàwǔ*
...in the evening	...晚上 *wǎnshàng*

一点
yīdiǎn
one o'clock

一点十分
yīdiǎnshífēn
ten past one

一点一刻
yīdiǎnyīkè
quarter past one

一点二十
yīdiǎnèrshí
twenty past one

一点半
yīdiǎnbàn
half past one

两点差一刻
liǎngdiǎn chà yīkè
quarter to two

两点差十分
liǎngdiǎn chà shífēn
ten to two

两点
liǎngdiǎn
two o'clock

It's noon/midnight

现在是中午/午夜
xiànzài shì zhōngwǔ /wǔyè

second

秒
miǎo

minute

分钟
fēnzhōng

hour

小时
xiǎoshí

a quarter of an hour

一刻钟
yīkèzhōng

half an hour

半小时
bànxiǎoshí

three-quarters of an hour

四十五分钟
sìshíwǔfēnzhōng

late

晚
wǎn

early

早
zǎo

soon

马上
mǎshàng

What time does it start?

几点开始?
jǐdiǎn kāishǐ

What time does it finish?

几点结束?
jǐdiǎn jiéshù

How long will it last?

要多久?
yào duōjiǔ

YOU MAY HEAR...

一会儿见	你来早了	你迟到了
yīhuìr jiàn	*nǐ láizǎo le*	*nǐ chídào le*
See you later	You're early	You're late

MAKING APPOINTMENTS

May I make an appointment?	我们可以定个见面时间吗? *wǒmen kěyǐ dìnggè jiànmiàn shíjiān ma*
Can we meet tomorrow?	我们可以明天见吗? *wǒmen kěyǐ míngtiānjiàn ma*
At 10 o'clock?	10点? *shídiǎn*
What time is best for you?	你什么时间合适? *nǐ shénme shíjiān héshì*
I'm sorry, I'm busy that day	对不起,我那天忙 *duìbuqǐ, wǒnàtiānmáng*
How about Tuesday?	星期二怎么样? *xīngqīèr zěnmeyàng*
In the morning/afternoon	在上午/下午 *zài shàngwǔ/ xiàwǔ*
That's fine for me	可以 *kěyǐ*
I'll see you then	到时候见 *dàoshíhòu jiàn*
I look forward to meeting you tomorrow	我期待着明天和你见面 *wǒ qīdàizhe míngtiān hénǐ jiànmiàn*

名片
míngpiàn
business card

碎纸机
suìzhǐjī
shredder

记事本
jìshìběn
note pad

公文包
gōngwénbāo
briefcase

AT THE MEETING

| I'm here... | 我来这儿... |
| | *wǒ láizhèr* |

| ...on business | ...谈生意 |
| | *tán shēngyì* |

| ...for a conference | ...出席研讨会 |
| | *chūxí yántǎohuì* |

| ...for a meeting | ...出席会议 |
| | *chūxí huìyì* |

| I have a meeting with... | 我和...有个会议 |
| | *wǒhé ...yǒugèhuìyì* |

| ...at two o'clock | ...在两点 |
| | *zài liǎngdiǎn* |

| I'm sorry I'm late | 对不起,我迟到了 |
| | *duìbuqǐ , wǒchídàole* |

| Here's my card | 这是我的名片 |
| | *zhèshì wǒde míngpiàn* |

| It's a pleasure to meet you | 很高兴见到你 |
| | *hěngāoxìng jiàndàonǐ* |

平板电脑
píngbǎndiànnǎo
tablet

打印机
dǎyìnjī
printer

YOU MAY HEAR...

你有预约吗?
nǐyǒu yùyuē ma
Have you got an appointment?

和谁?
héshuí
With whom?

在什么时候?
zài shénme shíhòu
At what time?

ESSENTIALS

THE WEATHER

What's the weather like?	天气怎么样? *tiānqì zěnmeyàng*
It's...	...天气 *tiānqì*
...good	很好... *hěnhǎo*
...bad	不好... *bùhǎo*
...warm	暖和... *nuǎnhuo*
...hot	热... *rè*
...cold	冷... *lěng*
...humid	潮湿... *cháoshī*

晴天
qíngtiān
It's sunny

下雨
xiàyǔ
It's raining

多云
duōyún
It's cloudy

暴风雨
bàofēngyǔ
It's stormy

What's the forecast?	天气预报怎么样？ *tiānqìyùbào zěnmeyàng*
What's the temperature?	气温怎么样？ *qìwēn zěnmeyàng*
It's...degrees	…度 *…dù*
It's a beautiful day	天气真好 *tiānqì zhēnhǎo*
The weather's changing	天气在变化 *tiānqì zài biànhuà*
Is it going to get colder/hotter?	会变冷/热吗？ *huì biàn lěng / rè ma*
It's cooling down	降温了 *jiàngwēn le*
Is it going to freeze?	会结冰吗？ *huì jiébīng ma*

下雪
xiàxuě
It's snowing

结冰
jiébīng
It's icy

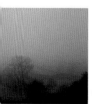

薄雾
bówù
It's misty

刮风
guāfēng
It's windy

GETTING AROUND

China has an excellent rail network, which links all the major cities and smaller towns, as well as an extensive bus system for long-distance travel. Most of the big cities have their own underground subway systems as well as taxis and public buses. Although you can rent a car in many cities, you can usually only drive within the city limits, and you may have to hire a driver if you wish to travel farther afield around this vast country.

ASKING WHERE THINGS ARE

Excuse me, please	对不起，请问
	duìbuqǐ, qǐngwèn
Where is...	...在哪儿
	zài nǎr
...the town center?	市中心...?
	shìzhōngxīn
...the train station?	火车站...?
	huǒchēzhàn
...a cash machine?	取款机...?
	qǔkuǎnjī
How do I get to...?	...怎么去?
	zěnmequ
I'm going to...	我去...
	wǒ qù
I'm looking for...	我在找...
	wǒ zàizhǎo
I'm lost	我走丢了
	wǒ zǒudiūle
Is it near?	近吗?
	jìnma
Is there a...nearby?	这附近有...吗?
	zhè fùjìn yǒu ...ma
Is it far?	远吗?
	yuǎnma
How far is...	...有多远?
	yǒuduōyuǎn
...the nearest bus stop?	最近的公共汽车站...?
	zuìjìnde gōnggòngqìchēzhàn
...the market?	自由市场...?
	zìyóushìcháng
Can I walk there?	我可以走着去么?
	wǒ kěyǐ zǒuzhe qùma

CAR AND BIKE RENTAL

Where is the car rental desk?	汽车出租柜台在哪儿? *qìchē chūzū guìtái zài nǎr*
I want to rent...	我想租... *wǒ xiǎngzū*
...a car	...一辆车 *yīliàng chē*
...a motorcycle	...一辆摩托车 *yīliàng mótuōchē*
...a bicycle	...一辆自行车 *yīliàng zìxíngchē*
for...days	租...天 *zū ...tiān*
for a week	租一星期 *zū yī xīngqī*

三厢轿车
sānxiāngjiàochē
sedan

掀背车
xiānbèichē
hatchback

摩托车
mótuōchē
motorcycle

小轮摩托
xiǎolúnmótuō
scooter

山地车
shāndìchē
mountain bike

公路车
gōnglùchē
road bike

for the weekend	租一个周末 *zū yīgè zhōumò*
I'd like......	我想要租一部... *wǒ xiǎngyào zū yíbù*
...an automatic	...自动挡的 *zìdòngdǎngde*
...a manual	...手动挡的 *shǒudòngdǎngde*
Has it got air conditioning?	有空调么? *yǒu kōngtiáo me*
Should I return it with a full tank?	还车时需要加满油么? *huánchēshí xūyào jiāmǎnyóu me*
Here's my driving license	这是我的驾驶执照 *zhèshì wǒde jiàshǐzhízhào*
When do I have to return it?	什么时候还? *shénme shíhòu huán*
Can I rent a GPS receiver?	我可以租卫星导航吗? *wǒ kěyǐ zū wèixīngdǎoháng ma*
Do you have a...	你有...吗 *nǐ yǒu...ma*

自行车头盔
zìxíngchē tóukuī
cycling helmet

气筒
qìtǒng
pump

锁
suǒ
lock

儿童座椅
értóng zuòyǐ
child seat

DRIVING

Is this the road to...?	这是去...的路吗?
	zhèshì qù ...de lù ma
Where is...	附近哪里有...
	fùjìn nǎlǐ yǒu
...the nearest garage?	...汽车修理站?
	qìchē xiūlǐzhàn
I'd like...	我想要...
	wǒ xiǎngyào
...some gas	...一些汽油
	yìxiē qìyóu
...40 liters of unleaded	...40升无铅汽油
	sìshí shēng wúqiānqìyóu
...30 liters of diesel	...30升柴油
	sānshí shēng cháiyóu
Fill it up, please	请加满
	qǐng jiāmǎn
Where do I pay?	我在哪儿付账?
	wǒ zài nǎr fùzhàng
The pump number is...	油泵号是...
	yóubèng hào shì
Can I pay by credit card?	我可以用信用卡付账吗?
	wǒ kěyǐ yòng xìnyòngkǎ fùzhàng ma
Do you have any change?	你有零钱吗?
	nǐ yǒu língqián ma
Please can you check...	请帮我检查...
	qǐng bāngwǒ jiǎnchá
...the oil	...机油
	jīyóu
...the tire pressure	...胎压
	tāiyā

PARKING

Is there a parking lot nearby?	这附近有停车场吗？ *zhè fùjìn yǒu tíngchēchǎng ma*
Can I park here?	这儿可以停车吗？ *zhèr kěyǐ tíngchē ma*
Is it free?	这是免费的吗？ *zhè shì miǎnfèi de ma*
How much does it cost?	这个多少钱？ *zhègè duōshǎoqián*
How much is it...	多少钱... *duōshǎoqián*
...per hour?	...每小时？ *měixiǎoshí*
...per day?	...每天？ *měitiān*
...overnight?	...一晚上？ *yīwǎnshàng*

车顶行李架
chēdǐngxínglǐjià
roofrack

儿童座椅
értóngzuòyǐ
child seat

加油站
jiāyóuzhàn
gas station

THE CAR

行李箱
xínglixiāng
trunk

排气管
páiqìguǎn
exhaust

车轮
chēlún
wheel

车门
chēmén
door

INSIDE THE CAR

座椅头枕
zuòyǐtóuzhěn
head rest

车门把手
chēménbǎshǒu
handle

前座
qiánzuò
front seat

门锁
ménsuǒ
door lock

安全带
ānquándài
seat belt

后座
hòuzuò
back seat

挡风玻璃
dǎngfēngbōli
windshield

引擎盖
yǐnqínggài
hood

前灯
qiándēng
headlight

保险杠
bǎoxiǎngàng
bumper

轮胎
lúntāi
tire

发动机
fādòngjī
engine

THE CONTROLS

汽车音响
qìchēyīnxiǎng
car stereo

警示灯
jǐngshìdēng
hazard lights

车速表
chēsùbiǎo
speedometer

安全气囊
ānquánqìnáng
airbag

仪表盘
yíbiǎopán
dashboard

取暖器
qǔnuǎnqì
heater

喇叭
lǎba
horn

变速杆
biànsùgǎn
gear shift

方向盘
fāngxiàngpán
steering wheel

ROAD SIGNS

单行
dānxíng
one way

出口
chūkǒu
exit

停
tíng
stop

禁入通行
jìnzhǐtōngxíng
no entry

禁止停车
jìnzhǐtíngchē
no parking

最高速度
zuìgāosùdù
maximum speed

路牌
lùpái
road name sign

ON THE ROAD

停车计时收费器
tíngchējìshíshōufèiqì
parking meter

交通信号灯
jiāotōngxìnhàodēng
traffic light

交通警察
jiāotōngjǐngchá
traffic police officer

机动三轮车
jīdòngsānlúnchē
motor rickshaw

地图
dìtú
map

机场专线
jīchǎngzhuānxiàn
airport bus sign

人行横道
rénxínghéngdào
pedestrian crossing

AT THE STATION

Where can I buy a ticket?	我在哪儿可以买到票? *wǒ zàinǎr kěyǐ mǎidào piào*
Is there an automatic ticket machine?	这儿有自动售票机吗? *zhèr yǒu zìdòng shòupiàojī ma*
How much is a ticket to...?	去...的票多少钱? *qù ...de piào duōshǎo qián*
Two tickets to...	两张去...的票 *liǎng zhāng qù ...de piào*
I'd like...	我想要 *wǒ xiǎngyào*
...a one-way ticket to...	...一张单程票去... *yīzhāng dānchéngpiào qù*
...a return ticket to...	...一张往返票去... *yīzhāng wǎngfǎnpiào qù*
I'd like to...	我想要... *wǒ xiǎngyào*
...reserve a seat...	...订座位 *dìng zuòwèi*
on the express to...	...在去...的特快上... *zài qù ...de tèkuài shàng*

票
piào
ticket

自动售票机
zìdòng shòupiàojī
automatic ticket machine

...book a sleeper berth	...订一个卧铺 *dìng yīgè wòpù*
Is there a reduction...	有减价的... *yǒu jiǎnjià de*
...for children?	...儿童票吗? *értóngpiào ma*
...for students?	...学生票吗? *xuéshēngpiào ma*
...for senior citizens?	...老年人优惠票吗? *lǎoniánrén yōuhuìpiào ma*
Is there a dining car?	有餐车么? *yǒu cānchē ma*
Is it a fast/slow train?	这是一趟高速/低速列车吗? *zhèshì yītàng gāosù / dīsù lièchē ma*
Is it a direct train?	这是一趟直达车吗? *zhèshì yītàng zhídá chē ma*
Do I stamp the ticket before boarding?	我在上车之前要检票吗? *wǒ zài shàngchē zhīqián yào jiǎnpiào ma*
For how long is the ticket valid?	票有效多长时间? *piào yǒuxiào duōcháng shíjiān*

YOU MAY HEAR...

列车从...站台发车
lièchē cóng ...zhàntái fāchē
The train leaves from platform...

你必须换乘列车
nǐ bìxū huànchéng lièchē
You must change trains

TRAVELING BY TRAIN

Do you have a timetable?	你有时刻表吗？ *nǐ yǒu shíkèbiǎo ma*
What time is...	什么时间... *shénme shíjiān*
...the next train to...?	下趟 去..的列车...？ *xiàtàng qù ..de lièchē*
...the last train to...?	去...的末班车... *qù ...de mòbānchē*
Which platform does it leave from?	从哪个站台发车？ *cóng nǎge zhàntái fāchē*
What time does it arrive in...?	什么时间到达...？ *shénme shíjiān dàodá*
How long does it take?	需要多长时间？ *xūyào duōcháng shíjiān*
Is this the train for...?	这是去...的列车吗？ *zhèshì qù ...de lièchē ma*
Is this the right platform for...?	这是...的站台吗？ *zhèshì ...de zhàntái ma*
Where is platform three?	3号站台在哪儿？ *sānhào zhàntái zài nǎr*
Does this train stop at...?	这趟列车在...停吗？ *zhètàng lièchē zài ...tíng ma*

YOU MAY HEAR...

你必须验证你的票
nǐ bìxū yànzhèng nǐdepiào
You must validate your ticket

请出示车票
qǐng chūshì chēpiào
Tickets, please

Where do I change for...?
我在哪儿换车去...?
wǒ zàinǎr huànchē qù

Is this seat free?
这个座位有人吗?
zhègè zuòwèi yǒurén ma

I've reserved this seat
我订了这个座位了
wǒ dìngle zhègè zuòwèi le

Do I get off here?
我在这儿下车吗?
wǒ zài zhèr xiàchē ma

Where is the subway station?
地铁站在哪儿?
dìtiězhàn zàinǎr

Which line goes to...?
哪条线去...?
nǎ tiáo xiàn qù

How many stops is it?
有多少站?
yǒu duōshǎo zhàn

Where are we?
我们在哪儿?
wǒmen zàinǎr

车站大厅
chēzhàndàtīng
concourse

列车
lièchē
train

餐车
cānchē
dining car

列车卧铺
lièchēwòpù
sleeper berth

BUSES

When is the next bus to...?	下辆去...的车什么时候来？ *xià liàng qù ...de chē shénme shíhòu lái*
What is the fare to...?	去...多少钱？ *qù ...duōshǎoqián*
Where is...	...在哪儿 *zàinǎr*
...the bus stop?	公共汽车站...？ *gōnggòngqìchēzhàn*
...the bus station?	公共汽车总站...？ *gōnggòngqìchēzǒngzhàn*
Is this the bus stop for...?	这是去...的公共汽车站吗？ *zhèshì qù ...de gōnggòngqìchē zhàn ma*
Does the number 4 stop here?	4路公共汽车在这儿停吗？ *sì lù gōnggòngqìchē zài zhèr tíng ma*
Where can I buy a ticket?	我在哪儿可以买到票？ *wǒ zàinǎr kěyǐ mǎidào piào*
Can I pay on the bus?	我可以在公共汽车上付钱吗？ *wǒ kěyǐ zài gōnggòngqìchē shàng fùqián ma*
Which buses go to the city center?	哪辆公共汽车去市中心？ *nǎ liàng gōnggòngqìchē qù shìzhōngxīn*

公共汽车
gōnggòngqìchē
bus

公共汽车总站
gōnggòngqìchēzǒngzhàn
bus station

TAXIS

Where can I get a taxi?	我在哪儿可以找到出租车？ *wǒ zàinǎr kěyǐ zhǎodào chūzūchē*
Can I order a taxi?	我可以订一辆出租车吗？ *wǒ kěyǐ dìng yīliàng chūzūchē ma*
I want a taxi to...	我想叫辆出租车去... *wǒ xiǎng jiào liàng chūzūchē qù*
Can you take me to...	你可以带我去... *nǐ kěyǐ dài wǒ qù*
Is it far?	远吗？ *yuǎn ma*
How long will it take?	要多长时间？ *yào duōcháng shíjiān*
How much will it cost?	多少钱？ *duōshǎoqián*
Can you drop me here?	你能把我放在这里吗？ *nǐ néng bǎ wǒ fàngzài zhèlǐ ma*
What do I owe you?	我该给你多少钱？ *wǒ gāi gěinǐ duōshǎoqián*
Keep the change	不用找了 *búyòngzhǎole*
May I have a receipt?	我能要一个收据吗？ *wǒ néng yào yīgè shōujù ma*
Please wait for me	请等我 *qǐng děng wǒ*

出租车
chūzūchē
taxi

出租车站
chūzūchēzhàn
taxi stand

BOATS

Are there any boat trips?	这有乘船游览项目吗? *zhè yǒu chéngchuányóulǎn xiàngmù ma*
Where does the boat leave from?	船从哪儿离开? *chuán cóngnǎr líkāi*
When is...	什么时候... *shénme shíhòu*
...the next ferry to...?	...下一班去...的渡船? *xiàyībān qù ...de dùchuán*
...the first boat?	...第一班船? *dìyībān chuán*
...the last boat?	...最后一班船? *zuìhòu yībān chuán*
I'd like two tickets for...	我想要两张...的票 *wǒ xiǎng yào liǎngzhāng ...de piào*
...the river trip	...游船 *yóuchuán*

渡船
dùchuán
ferry

水翼船
shuǐyìchuán
hydrofoil

游艇
yóutǐng
yacht

气垫船
qìdiànchuán
hovercraft

...the ferry service	...渡船服务 *dùchuán fúwù*
How much is it for...	多少钱... *duōshǎoqián*
...two people?	...两个人? *liǎnggè rén*
...a family?	...一家? *yìjiā*
...a cabin?	...包舱? *bāocāng*
Can I buy a ticket on board?	我可以在船上买票吗? *wǒ kěyǐ zài chuánshàng mǎipiào ma*
Is there wheelchair access?	这儿有轮椅通道吗? *zhèr yǒu lúnyǐtōngdào ma*
Can we eat on board?	我们可以在船上就餐吗? *wǒmen kěyǐ zài chuánshàng jiùcān ma*

游乐船
yóulèchuán
pleasure boat

救生圈
jiùshēngquān
life ring

双体船
shuāngtǐchuán
catamaran

救生衣
jiùshēngyī
life jacket

AIR TRAVEL

Which terminal do I need?	我需要去哪个候机楼？ *wǒ xūyào qù nǎge hòujīlóu*
Where do I check in?	我去哪儿办理登机手续？ *wǒ qùnǎr bànlǐ dēngjī shǒuxù*
Where is/are...	...在哪儿 *...zàinǎr*
...the arrivals hall?	抵达大厅...？ *dǐdá dàtīng...*
...the departures hall?	候机大厅...？ *hòujī dàtīng...*
...the boarding gate?	登机门...？ *dēngjīmén...*
I'm traveling...	我搭乘... *wǒ dāchéng*
...economy	...经济舱 *jīngjìcāng*
...business class	...商务舱 *shāngwùcāng*
Here is my...	这是我的... *zhè shì wǒde*

旅行袋
lǚxíngdài
duffel bag

护照
hùzhào
passport

飞机餐
fēijīcān
in-flight meal

登机牌
dēngjīpái
boarding pass

I'm checking in one suitcase

我需要办理1件行李托运
wǒ xūyào bànlǐ yíjiàn xíngli tuōyùn

I packed it myself

我自己整理的
wǒ zìjǐ zhěnglǐ de

I have one piece of hand luggage

我有一个手提行李
wǒ yǒu yīgè shǒutí xíngli

What is the weight allowance?

行李限重是多少?
xíngli xiànzhòng shì duōshǎo

How much is excess baggage?

超重行李怎么收费?
chāozhòng xíngli zěnme shōufèi

Will a meal be served?

提供飞机餐吗?
tígòng fēijīcān ma

I'd like...

我想要...
wǒ xiǎngyào

...a window seat

...一个靠窗座位
yīgè kàochuāng zuòwèi

...an aisle seat

...一个靠道座位
yīgè kàodào zuòwèi

...a bulkhead seat

...一个靠紧急出口的座位
yīgè kào jǐnjíchūkǒu de zuòwèi

YOU MAY HEAR...

请出示你的护照/机票.
qǐng chūshì nǐde hùzhào / jīpiào
Your passport/ticket please

这是你的包吗?
zhèshì nǐde bāo ma
Is this your bag?

AT THE AIRPORT

Here's my...	这是我的... *zhè shì wǒde*
...boarding pass	...登机牌 *dēngjīpái*
...passport	...护照 *hùzhào*
Can I change some money?	我可以兑换一些钱吗? *wǒ kěyǐ duìhuàn yìxiēqián ma*
What is the exchange rate?	汇率是多少? *huìlǜ shì duōshǎo*
Is the flight to...on time?	去...的航班准时吗? *qù...de hángbān zhǔnshí ma*
Is the flight delayed?	航班晚点了吗? *hángbān wǎndiǎn le ma*

办理登机手续
bànlǐ dēngjīshǒuxù
check-in

货币兑换点
huòbiduìhuàndiǎn
currency exchange booth

护照检查处
hùzhào jiǎncháchù
passport control

免税店
miǎnshuìdiàn
duty-free shop

领取行李处
lǐngqǔxínglǐchù
baggage claim

飞行员
fēixíngyuán
pilot

飞机
fēijī
airplane

空中小姐
kōngzhōngxiǎojiě
flight attendant

How late is it?	晚点了多久? *wǎndiǎn le duōjiǔ*
Which gate does flight...leave from?	航班...从哪个登机门登机? *hángbān ...cóng nǎge dēngjīmén dēngjī*
What time do I board?	我什么时候登机? *wǒ shénme shíhòu dēngjī*
Where are the carts?	行李车在哪儿? *xínglǐchē zàinǎr*
Here is the baggage claim tag	这是行李领取标签 *zhèshì xínglǐ lǐngqǔ biāoqiān*
I can't find my baggage	我找不到我的行李 *wǒ zhǎobúdào wǒde xínglǐ*

EATING OUT

It is easy to eat well and inexpensively in China. Not only can you choose from a wide range of Western-style cafés and traditional Chinese teahouses and restaurants, but you can also try many different regional cuisines, from the fiery dishes of Sichuan to traditional Peking duck and the dim sum of Cantonese cooking. Chinese people usually eat early, so lunch is served from 11am onwards and dinner from 5pm.

MAKING A RESERVATION

I'd like to book a table...	我想订一桌座位... *wǒxiǎng dìng yìzhuō zuòwèi*
...for lunch/dinner	...来吃午餐/晚餐 *lái chī wǔcān / wǎncān*
...for four people	...4个人 *sìgèrén*
...for this evening at seven	...今天晚上7点来用餐 *jīntiān wǎnshàng qīdiǎn lái yòngcān*
...for tomorrow at noon	...明天中午来用餐 *míngtiān zhōngwǔ lái yòngcān*
...for lunchtime today	...今天午餐时间来用餐 *jīntiān wǔcān shíjiān lái yòngcān*
Do you have a table earlier/later?	早/晚一点儿有位子吗? *zǎo / wǎn yìdiǎnr yǒu wèizi ma*
My name is...	我的名字是... *wǒde míngzì shì*
My telephone number is...	我的电话号码是... *wǒde diànhuàhàomǎ shì*
I have a reservation	我有预订 *wǒ yǒu yùdìng*
...in the name of...	...用...的名字 *yòng ...de míngzì*
We haven't booked	我们没有预订 *wǒmen méiyǒu yùdìng*
May we sit here?	我们可以坐在这里吗? *wǒmen kěyǐ zuòzài zhèlǐ ma*
May we sit outside?	我们可以坐在外面吗? *wǒmen kěyǐ zuòzài wàimiàn ma*
I'm waiting for someone	我在等人 *wǒzài děngrén*

ORDERING A MEAL

May we see...	我们可以看一下... *wǒmen kěyǐ kànyīxià*
...the menu?	...菜单吗? *càidān ma*
...the wine list?	...酒单吗? *jiǔdān ma*
Do you have...	你有... *nǐ yǒu*
...a set menu?	...套餐菜单吗? *...tàocān càidān ma*
...a fixed-price menu?	...固定价格菜单吗? *...gùdìng jiàgé càidān ma*
...a children's menu?	...儿童菜单吗? *...értóng càidān ma*
...an à la carte menu	...单点的菜单吗? *...dāndiǎn de càidān ma*
What are today's specials?	今天的特色菜都有哪些? *jīntiān de tèsècài dōuyǒu nǎxiē*
What do you recommend?	你推荐哪些? *nǐtuījiàn nǎxiē*

YOU MAY HEAR...

你有预订吗?
nǐyǒu yùdìng ma
Do you have a reservation?

请坐
qǐngzuò
Please be seated

用什么名字订的?
yòng shénme míngzì dìng de
In what name?

可以点菜了吗?
kěyǐ diǎncài le ma
Are you ready to order?

What is this?	这是什么？ *zhè shì shénme*
Are there any vegetarian dishes?	有素食吗？ *yǒu sùshí ma*
I can't eat...	我不能吃... *wǒ bùnéng chī*
...dairy foods	...乳制品 *...rǔzhìpǐn*
...nuts	...坚果 *jiānguǒ*
...wheat	...小麦 *xiǎomài*
To start, I'll have...	我要...作为开胃菜 *wǒyào ...zuòwéi kāiwèicài*
May we have...	我们可以要... *wǒmen kěyǐyào...*
...some noodles?	...一些面条吗？ *...yīxiē miàntiáo ma*
...the dessert menu?	...餐后甜点菜单吗？ *...cānhòu tiándiǎn càidān ma*

READING THE MENU...

开胃菜
kāiwèicài
appetizers

主菜
zhǔcài
main courses

米饭/面条
mǐfàn/miàntiáo
rice/noodles

头道菜
tóudàocài
first courses

蔬菜
shūcài
vegetables

餐后甜点
cānhòutiándiǎn
desserts

COMPLAINING

I didn't order this	我没有点这个 *wǒ méiyǒu diǎn zhège*
You forgot my dessert	你忘了我的餐后甜点了 *nǐ wàngle wǒde cānhòu tiándiǎn le*
I can't wait any longer	我不能再等了 *wǒ bùnéng zàiděng le*

PAYING

That was delicious	很好吃 *hěn hǎochī*
The check, please	请给我账单 *qǐng gěiwǒ zhàngdān*
May I have...	我可以要... *wǒ kěyǐ yào*
...a receipt?	...一个收据吗? *yīgè shōujù ma*
...an itemized bill?	...一个有消费明细的账单吗? *yīgè yǒu xiāofèimíngxì de zhàngdān ma*
Is service included?	含服务费吗? *hán fúwùfèi ma*
There's a mistake here	这里有个错误 *zhèlǐ yǒugè cuòwù*

YOU MAY HEAR...

我们不接受信用卡
wǒmen bù jiēshòu xìnyòngkǎ
We don't take credit cards

请输入你的密码
qǐng shūrù nǐde mìmǎ
Please enter your PIN

DISHES AND CUTLERY

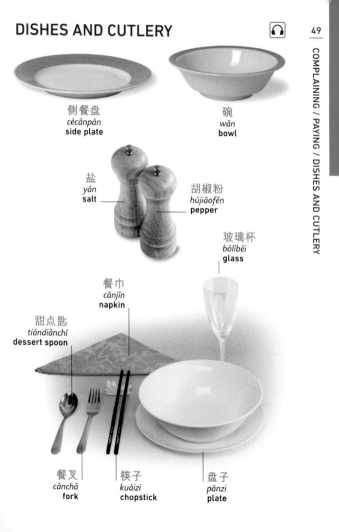

侧餐盘
cècānpán
side plate

碗
wǎn
bowl

盐
yán
salt

胡椒粉
hújiāofěn
pepper

玻璃杯
bōlíbēi
glass

餐巾
cānjīn
napkin

甜点匙
tiándiǎnchí
dessert spoon

餐叉
cānchā
fork

筷子
kuàizi
chopstick

盘子
pánzi
plate

AT THE CAFÉ OR BAR

The menu, please	请给我菜单 *qǐng gěiwǒ càidān*
Do you have...?	你们有...吗？ *nǐmen yǒu...ma*
What fruit juices do you have?	你们有哪些果汁？ *nǐmen yǒu nǎxiē guǒzhī*
I'd like...	我想要... *wǒ xiǎngyào*
I'll have...	我点... *wǒdiǎn*

加牛奶的咖啡
jiā niúnǎi de kāfēi
coffee with milk

黑咖啡
hēikāfēi
black coffee

奶茶
nǎichá
tea with milk

绿茶
lǜchá
green tea

YOU MAY HEAR...

你想要点儿什么？
nǐ xiǎng yàodiǎnr shénme
What would you like?

还要别的吗？
háiyào biéde ma
Anything else?

就这些吗？
jiù zhèxiē ma
Will that be all?

柠檬茶
níngméngchá
tea with lemon

红茶
hóngchá
black tea

花茶
huāchá
flower tea

普尔茶
pǔ'ěrchá
pu'er tea

A cup of...	一杯... *yìbēi*
A bottle of...	一瓶... *yìpíng*
A glass of...	一杯... *yìbēi*
With lemon/milk	加柠檬/牛奶 *jiā níngméng / niúnǎi*
With sugar	加糖 *jiā táng*
Another...please	请再来一份... *qǐng zàilái yìfèn*
The same again, please	请照样再来一份 *qǐng zhàoyàng zàilái yìfèn*
How much is that?	多少钱? *duōshǎoqián*

CAFÉ AND BAR DRINKS

菠萝汁
bōluózhī
pineapple juice

苹果汁
píngguǒzhī
apple juice

橙汁
chéngzhī
orange juice

柠檬水
níngméngshuǐ
lemonade

可乐
kělè
cola

番茄汁
fānqiézhī
tomato juice

椰奶饮品
yēnǎi yǐnpǐn
coconut milk drink

橘子汁
júzizhī
orangeade

茶和咖啡饮品
chá hé kāfēiyǐnpǐn
tea and coffee drink

冰绿茶
bīnglǜchá
iced green tea

饮用水
yǐnyòngshuǐ
tap water

瓶装矿泉水
píngzhuāngkuàngquánshuǐ
bottle of mineral water

啤酒
píjiǔ
beer

米酒
mǐjiǔ
rice wine

红酒
hóngjiǔ
red wine

白葡萄酒
báipútáojiǔ
white wine

YOU MAY HEAR...

瓶装的
píngzhuāngde
Bottled?

不带气的还是带气的?
búdàiqìde háishì dàiqìde
Still or sparkling?

加冰吗　加柠檬吗
jiābīng ma　*jiā níngméng ma*
With ice?　With lemon?

BAR SNACKS

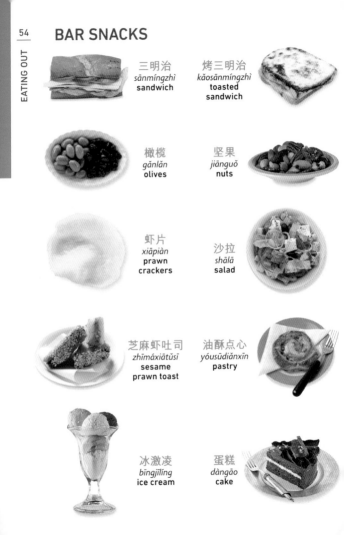

三明治
sānmíngzhì
sandwich

烤三明治
kǎosānmíngzhì
toasted
sandwich

橄榄
gǎnlǎn
olives

坚果
jiānguǒ
nuts

虾片
xiāpiàn
prawn
crackers

沙拉
shālā
salad

芝麻虾吐司
zhīmáxiātǔsī
sesame
prawn toast

油酥点心
yóusūdiǎnxīn
pastry

冰激凌
bīngjīlíng
ice cream

蛋糕
dàngāo
cake

FAST FOOD

May I have...	我可以要一个... *wǒ kěyǐ yàoyīgè*
...to eat in/carry out	...在里面就餐/带走 *zài lǐmiàn jiùcān / dàizǒu*
...some ketchup/mustard	...一些番茄酱/芥末酱 *yīxiē fānqiéjiàng / jièmojiàng*

汉堡包
hànbǎobāo
hamburger

鸡肉汉堡
jīròuhànbǎo
chicken burger

沙爹鸡肉串
shādiējīròuchuàn
chicken satay skewers

热狗
règǒu
hot dog

烤肉串
kǎoròuchuàn
kebab

薯条
shǔtiáo
French fries

炸鸡
zhájī
fried chicken

比萨饼
bǐsàbǐng
pizza

BREAKFAST

May I have some...	我可以要一点儿... *wǒkěyǐ yào yìdiǎnr*
...sugar?	...糖吗？ *táng ma*
...milk?	...牛奶吗？ *niúnǎi ma*
...artificial sweetener?	...人造甜味剂吗？ *rénzào tiánwèijì ma*
...butter?	...黄油吗？ *huángyóu ma*
...jam?	...果酱吗？ *guǒjiàng ma*
...decaf coffee?	...无咖啡因咖啡吗？ *wúkāfēiyīn kāfēi ma*

咖啡
kāfēi
coffee

茶
chá
tea

热巧克力
rèqiǎokèlì
hot chocolate

橙汁
chéngzhī
orange juice

苹果汁
píngguǒzhī
apple juice

面包
miànbāo
bread

小圆面包
xiǎo yuánmiànbāo
bread roll

烤面包
kǎomiànbāo
toast

谷类食品
gǔlèi shípǐn
cereal

橘子酱
júzijiàng
marmalade

蜂蜜
fēngmì
honey

炒鸡蛋
chǎojīdàn
scrambled eggs

煮鸡蛋
zhǔjīdàn
boiled egg

荷包蛋
hébāodàn
poached egg

果味酸奶
guǒwèisuānnǎi
fruit yogurt

鲜果
xiānguǒ
fresh fruit

FIRST COURSES

汤
tāng
soup

肉汤/清汤
ròutāng/qīngtāng
broth/clear soup

鸡蛋汤
jīdàn tāng
**egg drop
soup**

木耳肉片姜汤
*mùěrròupiàn
jiāngtāng*
**ginger soup with
pork and wood
ear mushrooms**

饺子
jiǎozi
dumplings

馒头
mántou
steamed bun

蟹钳
xièqián
**stuffed
crab claws**

酸菜
suāncài
**pickled
cabbage**

春卷
chūnjuǎn
spring rolls

凤爪
fèngzhǎo
chicken feet

煎蛋饼
jiāndànbǐng
omelet

虾佐豆腐皮
xiāzuǒdòufupí
shrimp in
beancurd skin

叉烧包
chāshāobāo
BBQ pork
buns

酱汁培根和香肠
*jiàngzhī péigēn hé
xiāngchǎng*
soy-cured bacon
and sausages

豆豉
dòuchǐ
fermented
black beans

猪肉烧麦
zhūròushāomài
pork
dumplings

排骨
páigǔ
spare
ribs

海鲜酱猪肉
hǎixiānjiàngzhūròu
Hoisin pork

炸馄饨
zháhúntun
wontons

脆皮北京鸭
cuìpíběijīngyā
crispy Peking
duck

MAIN COURSES

I would like...	我想要... *wǒxiǎngyào*	...the shellfish	...贝类 *bèilèi*
...the lamb	...羊肉 *yángròu*	...the shrimp	...虾 *xiā*
...the pork	...猪肉 *zhūròu*	...the crab	螃蟹 *pángxiè*
...the spare ribs	...排骨 *páigǔ*	...the lobster	...龙虾 *lóngxiā*
...the beef	...牛肉 *niúròu*	...the vegetables	...蔬菜 *shūcài*
...the steak	...牛排 *niúpái*	...the tofu	...豆腐 *dòufu*
...the chicken	...鸡肉 *jīròu*	...roasted	...烤的 *kǎode*
...the duck	...鸭肉 *yāròu*	...stir-fried	...炒的 *chǎode*
...sizzling	...油煎的 *yóujiānde*	...fried	...炸的 *zháde*

YOU MAY SEE...

海鲜
hǎixiān
shellfish

鱼
yú
fish

YOU MAY HEAR...

你的牛排要怎么做？
nǐde niúpái yào zěnmezuò
How do you like your steak?

一分熟还是三分熟？
yìfēnshú háishì sānfēnshú
Rare or medium rare?

要完全煎熟吗？
yào wánquán jiānshú ma
Well done?

...steamed	...清蒸的 *qīngzhēngde*	...broiled	...烤的 *kǎode*
...boiled	...煮的 *zhǔde*	...raw	...生的 *shēngde*

禽肉
qínròu
poultry

肉
ròu
meat

MAIN COURSE DISHES

豉汁炒虾
chǐzhī chǎoxiā
**shrimp in mixed
bean sauce**

鲍鱼蘑菇
bàoyú mógu
**snails with
mushrooms**

糖醋鱼
tángcùyú
**fish with sweet
and sour sauce**

油爆虾
yóubào xiā
**stir-fried
shrimp**

姜汁龙虾
jiāngzhī lóngxiā
**lobster with
ginger**

宫保鸡丁
gōngbǎo jīdīng
**Kung Pao
chicken**

豉汁鸡
chǐzhījī
**chicken in
black bean
sauce**

清蒸鸭
qīngzhēngyā
**steamed
duck**

小锅蒸鸡
xiǎoguō zhēngjī
**steam-pot
chicken**

棒棒鸡
bàngbàngjī
**bang bang
chicken**

糖醋猪肉
tángcùzhūròu
**sweet and
sour pork**

珍珠猪肉丸
*zhēnzhū
zhūròuwán*
**pearly pork
balls**

猪肉丸
zhūròuwán
pork meatballs

冰糖猪肘
bīngtángzhūzhǒu
**crystal sugar
pork knuckle**

桔皮牛肉
júpíniúròu
**beef with
tangerine rind**

葱爆羊羔肉
*cōngbào
yánggāoròu*
**lamb with
scallions**

VEGETABLES AND SIDE DISHES

沙拉
shālā
salad

蒸菜
zhēngcài
steamed
vegetables

泡菜
pàocài
pickled
vegetables

炒杂菜
chǎo zácài
stir-fried
vegetables

蘑菇
mógu
stuffed
mushrooms

米饭
mǐfàn
rice

薯条
shǔtiáo
French
fries

星洲炒米
xīngzhōuchǎomǐ
Singapore
noodles

炒面
chǎomiàn
stir-fried
noodles

炒饭
chǎofàn
fried rice

DESSERTS

果汁冰糕
guǒzhī bīnggāo
sherbet

冰激凌
bīngjīlíng
ice cream

蛋糕
dàngāo
cake

水果沙拉
shuǐguǒ shālā
fruit salad

杏仁豆腐
xìngrén dòufu
almond bean curd

拔丝苹果
básī píngguǒ
apples in hot toffee

八宝米布丁
bābǎomǐbùdīng
eight treasure rice pudding

果馅油炸饼
guǒxiàn yóuzhábǐng
fruit fritters

花生蛋糕
huāshēng dàngāo
peanut cake

红豆沙
hóngdòushā
sweet red bean paste

PLACES TO STAY

China offers the visitor a wide range of places to stay, with something to suit everyone's personal preferences and budget. These range from luxurious four- and five-star hotels, managed by international and Chinese chains, to traditional Chinese spas, budget hotels, and even youth hostels. Although you cannot go camping in China, you can rent an apartment for longer stays.

MAKING A RESERVATION

I'd like...	我想... *wǒxiǎng*
...to make a reservation	...预订 *yùdìng*
...a double room	...双人间 *shuāngrénjiān*
...a room with two twin beds	...双床间 *shuāngchuángjiān*
...a single room	...单人间 *dānrénjiān*
...a family room	...家庭间 *jiātíngjiān*
...a disabled person's room	...残疾人房间 *cánjírén fángjiān*
...with a bathtub/shower	...有浴室/淋浴的 *yǒu yùshì / línyùde*
...with a sea view	...能看到海景的 *néng kàndào hǎijǐng de*
...for two nights	...住两个晚上 *zhù liǎnggè wǎnshàng*
...for a week	...住一个星期 *zhù yīgè xīngqī*
Is breakfast included?	...包早餐吗? *bāo zǎocān ma*
How much is it...	多少钱... *duōshǎoqián*
...per night?	...一晚? *yīwǎn*
...per week?	...一周? *yīzhōu*
...with air-conditioning?	有空调的...? *yǒu kōngtiáo de*

CHECKING IN

I have a reservation in the name of...
我有一个以...登记的预订
wǒ yǒu yīgè yǐ ...dēngjì de yùdìng

Do you have...
有没有...
yǒuméiyǒu

I'd like...
我想要...
wǒxiǎngyào

...the keys for room...
...房间的钥匙
fángjiān de yàoshi

...a wake-up call at...
...唤醒服务在...点
huànxǐng fúwù zài ...diǎn

What time is...
什么时候...
shénme shíhòu

...breakfast?
...用早餐？
yòng zǎocān

...dinner?
...用晚餐？
yòng wǎncān

搬运工
bānyùngōng
porter

小冰箱
xiǎo bīngxiāng
mini bar

房间送餐服务
fángjiān sòngcān fúwù
room service

电梯
diàntī
elevators

IN YOUR ROOM

Do you have...
你有...吗
nǐyǒu ...ma

another...
另一个...
lìngyīgè

some more...
多一些...
duōyìxiē

I've lost my key
我丢了我的钥匙
wǒ diūle wǒde yàoshi

毯子
tǎnzi
blankets

枕头
zhěntou
pillows

插头转换器
chātóu zhuǎnhuànqì
adapter

灯泡
dēngpào
light bulb

YOU MAY HEAR...

你的房间号码是...
nǐde fángjiān hàomǎ shì
Your room number is...

这是你的钥匙.
zhèshì nǐde yàoshi
Here is your key

IN THE HOTEL

The room is...	房间... *fángjiān*
...too hot	...太热 *tàirè*
...too cold	...太冷 *tàilěng*
The TV doesn't work	电视机坏了 *diànshìjī huàile*
The window won't open	那个窗户打不开 *nàge chuānghù dǎbùkāi*
What is the code for the wifi?	无线网络的密码是什么? *wúxiànwǎngluò de mìmǎ shì shénme?*

电水壶
diànshuǐhú
kettle

散热器
sànrèqì
radiator

自动调温器
zìdòng tiáowēnqì
thermostat

单人间
dānrénjiān
single room

双人间
shuāngrénjiān
double room

房间号
fángjiānhào
room number

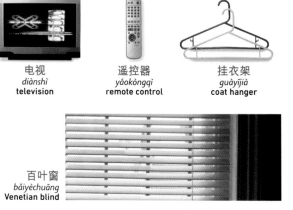

电视
diànshì
television

遥控器
yáokòngqì
remote control

挂衣架
guàyījià
coat hanger

百叶窗
bǎiyèchuāng
Venetian blind

CHECKING OUT

When do I have to vacate the room?	我什么时候得腾房? *wǒ shénmeshíhòu děi téngfáng*
Is there a porter to carry my bags?	有搬运工来搬我的行李吗? *yǒu bānyùngōng lái bān wǒde xíngli ma*
May I have the bill please?	我可以结帐吗? *wǒ kěyǐ jiézhàng ma*
Can I pay...	我可以用... *wǒ kěyǐ yòng*
...by credit card?	...信用卡付账吗? *xìnyòngkǎ fùzhàng ma*
...cash?	...现金付账吗? *xiànjīn fùzhàng ma*
I'd like a receipt	我想要一个收据 *wǒ xiǎngyào yīgè shōujù*

IN THE BATHROOM

毛巾
máojīn
towels

浴袍
yùpáo
bathrobe

肥皂
féizào
soap

除臭剂
chúchòujì
deodorant

牙膏
yágāo
toothpaste

泡浴液
pàoyùyè
bubblebath

净身盆
jìngshēnpén
bidet

沐浴乳
mùyùrǔ
shower gel

浴缸
yùgāng
bathtub

润肤露
rùnfūlù
body lotion

牙刷
yáshuā
toothbrush

吹风机
chuīfēngjī
blow-dryer

电动剃须刀
diàndòng tìxūdāo
electric razor

剃须泡沫
tìxū pàomò
shaving foam

剃须刀
tìxūdāo
razor

漱口液
shùkǒuyè
mouthwash

洗发水
xǐfàshuǐ
shampoo

护发素
hùfàsù
conditioner

指甲刀
zhǐjiǎdāo
nail clippers

指甲剪
zhǐjiǎjiǎn
nail scissors

May I have...
可以给我...
kěyǐ gěiwǒ

...the key please?
...钥匙吗?
yàoshi ma

...an extra bed?
...加一个床吗?
jiā yīgè chuáng ma

...a child's bed?
...一个儿童床吗?
yīgè értóngchuáng ma

...more cutlery?
...多点儿餐具吗?
duōdiǎnr cānjù ma

...more dishes?
...多点儿碗碟吗?
duōdiǎnr wǎndié ma

Where is...
...在哪儿?
zàinǎr

...the fusebox?
保险丝盒...
bǎoxiǎnsīhé

对流式电暖器
duìliúshì diànnuǎnqì
space heater

风扇
fēngshàn
fan

婴儿床
yīng'érchuáng
crib

高脚椅
gāojiǎoyǐ
high chair

...the water valve?	...水开关? *shuǐkāiguān*
...the supermarket?	...超级市场? *chāojíshìchǎng*
...the nearest store?	...最近的商店? *zuìjìn de shāngdiàn*
Is there a babysitting service?	这儿有保姆服务吗? *zhèr yǒu bǎomǔ fúwù ma*
How does the heating work?	怎么使用暖气? *zěnme shǐyòng nuǎnqì*
Is there...	这儿有... *zhèr yǒu*
...air-conditioning?	...空调吗? *kōngtiáo ma*
...central heating?	...中央供暖吗? *zhōngyānggòngnuǎn ma*
When does the cleaner come?	清洁工什么时候来? *qīngjiégōng shénmeshíhòu lái*
Where do I put the garbage?	垃圾需要放在哪里? *lājī xūyào fàngzài nǎlǐ*
Do you allow pets?	你们允许宠物吗? *nǐmen yǔnxǔ chǒngwù ma*

狗
gǒu
dog

PROBLEM SOLVING 🎧

Is there an inventory?	有货物清单吗？ *yǒu huòwù qīngdān ma*
Where is this item?	这件物品在哪儿？ *zhèjiàn wùpǐn zàinǎr*
I need...	我需要... *wǒ xūyào*
...an adapter	...一个插头转换器 *yīgè chātóu zhuǎnhuànqì*
...an extension cord	...一个电源延长线 *yīgè diànyuán yánchángxiàn*
...a flashlight	...一个手电筒 *yīgè shǒudiàntǒng*
...matches	...火柴 *huǒchái*

微波炉
wēibōlú
microwave

熨斗
yùndǒu
iron

熨衣板
yùnyībǎn
ironing board

拖把和水桶
tuōbǎ hé shuǐtǒng
mop and bucket

簸箕和短柄扫帚
bòjī hé duǎnbǐngsàozhou
dustpan and brush

清洁剂
qīngjiéjì
detergent

The shower doesn't work | 淋浴设施坏了
línyù shèshī huàile

The toilet is leaking | 厕所漏水
cèsuǒ lòushuǐ

Can you fix it today? | 你可以今天修吗?
nǐ kěyǐ jīntiān xiū ma

There's no... | 这儿没有...
zhèr méiyǒu

...electricity | ...电
diàn

...gas | ...煤气
méiqì

...water | ...水
shuǐ

洗衣机
xǐyījī
washing machine

冰箱
bīngxiāng
refrigerator

灭火器
mièhuǒqì
fire extinguisher

锁和钥匙
suǒ hé yàoshi
lock and key

烟雾警报器
yānwù jǐngbàoqì
smoke alarm

垃圾桶
lājītǒng
trash can

KITCHEN EQUIPMENT

烤盘
kǎopán
cookie sheet

案板
ànbǎn
cutting board

打蛋器
dǎdànqì
whisk

厨刀
chúdāo
kitchen knife

削皮刀
xuēpídāo
peeler

开罐器
kāiguànqì
can opener

开瓶器
kāipíngqì
bottle opener

拔塞钻
básāizuàn
corkscrew

切丝切片器
qiēsīqiēpiànqì
grater

木勺
mùsháo
wooden spoon

煎锅
jiānguō
frying pan

滤锅
lùguō
colander

抹刀
mǒdāo
spatula

长柄深平底锅
chángbǐngshēnpíngdǐguō
saucepan

烤架盘
kǎojiàpán
griddle pan

砂锅
shāguō
casserole dish

搅拌容器
jiǎobàn róngqì
mixing bowl

烤箱手套
kǎoxiāng shǒutào
oven mitts

围裙
wéiqún
apron

搅拌机
jiǎobànjī
blender

SHOPPING

As well as small shops, street bazaars, and bustling markets, there are department stores and shopping malls in many cities, where you can buy a wide range of goods. Most stores open between 8.30am and 8pm in summer but may stay open longer in winter. Many do not accept credit cards.

IN THE STORE

I'm looking for...	我在找... *wǒzàizhǎo*
Do you have...?	你有...吗? *nǐyǒu...ma*
I'm just looking	我只是随便看看 *wǒ zhǐshì suíbiàn kànkan*
I'm being served	有人为我服务了 *yǒurén wèiwǒ fúwù le*
Do you have any more of these?	这些还有么? *zhèxiē hái yǒu me*
How much is this?	这个多少钱? *zhègè duōshǎoqián*
Have you anything cheaper?	有便宜点的么? *yǒu piányidiǎn de me*
I'll take this one	我买这个 *wǒ mǎi zhègè*
Where can I pay?	在哪儿付账? *zài nǎr fùzhàng*
I'll pay...	我付... *wǒfù*
...in cash	...现金 *xiànjīn*
...by credit card	...信用卡 *xìnyòngkǎ*
May I have a receipt?	可以给我一个收据么? *kěyǐ gěiwǒ yīgè shōujù me*
I'd like to exchange this	我想换这个 *wǒxiǎng huàn zhège*
May I have a refund?	可以要求退款吗? *kěyǐ yāoqiú tuìkuǎn ma*

IN THE BANK

I'd like...
我想...
wǒxiǎng

...to change some money
...换点儿钱
huàn diǎnr qián

...into renminbi
...换人民币
huàn rénmínbì

...into dollars/sterling
...换美元/英镑
huàn měiyuán/yīngbàng

Here is my passport
这是我的护照
zhèshì wǒde hùzhào

My name is...
我叫...
wǒjiào

My account number is...
我的帐号是...
wǒde zhànghào shì

My bank details are...
我的银行资料是...
wǒde yínhángzīliào shì

护照
hùzhào
passport

钱
qián
money

汇率
huìlǜ
exchange rate

Can I withdraw money on my credit card?	我能用信用卡取钱么? *wǒnéngyòng xìnyòngkǎ qǔqián ma*
Do I have...	我要... *wǒyào*
...to key in my PIN?	...输入密码么? *shūrù mìmǎ ma*
...to sign here?	...在这儿签名么? *zàizhèr qiānmíng ma*
Is there a cash machine here?	这里有取款机么? *zhèlǐ yǒu qǔkuǎnjī ma*
The cash machine has taken my card	取款机吞了我的卡 *qǔkuǎnjī tūnle wǒdekǎ*
Has my money arrived yet?	我的钱到了么? *wǒdeqián dàole me*
When does the bank open/close?	银行什么时候开门/关门? *yínháng shénmeshíhòu kāimén / guānmén*

取款机
qǔkuǎnjī
cash machine

信用卡
xìnyòngkǎ
credit card

支票本
zhīpiàoběn
checkbook

STORES

百货商店
bǎihuòshāngdiàn
department store

纪念品店
jìniànpǐndiàn
souvenir shop

花店
huādiàn
florist

服装店
fúzhuāngdiàn
boutique

五金店
wǔjīndiàn
hardware store

书店
shūdiàn
bookstore

超市
chāoshì
supermarket

首饰店
shǒushìdiàn
jewelry store

蛋糕店
dàngāodiàn
cake shop

面包店
miànbāodiàn
bakery

水产店
shuǐchǎndiàn
fish seller

豆腐店
dòufudiàn
tofu shop

蔬菜店
shūcàidiàn
greengrocery

酒类专卖店
jiǔlèi zhuānmàidiàn
liquor store

肉店
ròudiàn
butcher

熟食店
shúshídiàn
delicatessen

AT THE MARKET

I would like...	我想要... *wǒ xiǎngyào*
How much is this?	多少钱? *duōshǎoqián*
It's too expensive	太贵了 *tàiguìle*
Do you have anything cheaper?	有便宜的么? *yǒupiányide ma*
That's fine, I'll take it	好,我买了 *hǎo, wǒmǎile*
I'll take...	我要... *wǒyào*
A kilo of...	一公斤... *yīgōngjīn*
Half a kilo of...	一斤... *yìjīn*
A little more, please	请再给我一些 *qǐng zài gěiwǒ yīxiē*
May I taste it?	我能尝尝么? *wǒ néng chángchang ma*
That's very good. I'll take some	很好,我要一些 *hěnhǎo ,wǒ yào yīxiē*
That will be all, thank you	就这些,谢谢 *jiù zhèxiē ,xièxie*

YOU MAY HEAR...

我能帮你么?
wǒnéng bāngnǐ ma
May I help you?

还有别的么?
háiyǒu biédema
Is there
anything else?

你想要多少?
nǐxiǎngyào duōshǎo
How much would
you like?

IN THE SUPERMARKET

Where is/are...	...在哪儿? *zài nǎr*
...the frozen foods?	冷冻食品... *lěngdòngshípǐn*
...the beverage aisle?	饮料类... *yǐnliàolèi*
...the checkout?	收银处... *shōuyínchù*
I'm looking for...	我在找... *wǒ zàizhǎo*

推车
tuīchē
grocery cart

购物篮
gòuwùlán
basket

Do you have any more?	你们还有么? *nǐmen háiyǒuma*
Is this reduced?	这个减价么? *zhège jiǎnjià ma*
Can you help me pack?	能帮我装么? *néng bāngwǒ zhuāng ma*
Where do I pay?	我在哪儿付款? *wǒ zàinǎr fùkuǎn*
Shall I key in my PIN?	我要输入密码么? *wǒ yào shūrù mìmǎ ma*
May I have a bag, please?	能给我一个袋子么? *néng gěiwǒ yīgèdàizi ma*

FRUIT

橙子
chéngzi
orange

柠檬
níngméng
lemon

桃
táo
peach

油桃
yóutáo
nectarine

青柠
qīngníng
lime

樱桃
yīngtáo
cherries

杏
xìng
apricot

梅子
méizi
plum

葡萄柚
pútáoyòu
grapefruit

荔枝
lìzhī
lychee

草莓
cǎoméi
strawberry

番石榴
fānshíliu
guava

瓜
guā
melon

葡萄
pútáo
grapes

香蕉
xiāngjiāo
banana

石榴
shíliú
pomegranate

苹果
píngguǒ
apple

梨
lí
pear

菠萝
bōluó
pineapple

芒果
mángguǒ
mango

VEGETABLES

土豆
tŭdòu
potato

胡萝卜
húluóbo
carrot

青椒
qīngjiāo
pepper

辣椒
làjiāo
chili peppers

茄子
qiézi
eggplant

西红柿
xīhóngshì
tomato

洋葱
yángcōng
onion

大蒜
dàsuàn
garlic

葱
cōng
scallion

韭葱
jiŭcōng
leek

蘑菇
mógu
mushroom

荸荠
bíqí
water
chestnuts

豌豆
wāndòu
garden
peas

四季豆
sìjìdòu
green
beans

小白菜
xiǎobáicài
bok
choy

白菜
báicài
Chinese
cabbage

菠菜
bōcài
spinach

西兰花
xīlánhuā
broccoli

卷心菜
juǎnxīncài
cabbage

豆芽
dòuyá
bean sprouts

MEAT AND POULTRY

May I have...	可以给我... *kěyǐgěiwǒ*
...a slice of...?	...一片...? *yīpiàn*
...a piece of...?	...一块...? *yīkuài*
That's enough!	够了! *gòule*

火腿
huǒtuǐ
ham

牛肉馅
niúròuxiànr
ground beef

牛排
niúpái
steak

猪肉
zhūròu
pork

排骨
páigǔ
spare ribs

羊肉
yángròu
lamb

鸡肉
jīròu
chicken

鸭肉
yāròu
duck

FISH AND SHELLFISH

鲤鱼
lǐyú
carp

鳕鱼
xuěyú
cod

海鲈
hǎilú
sea bass

鲈鱼
lúyú
sea perch

剑鱼
jiànyú
swordfish

鱿鱼
yóuyú
squid

螃蟹
pángxiè
crab

龙虾
lóngxiā
lobster

扇贝
shànbèi
scallops

虾
xiā
shrimp

BREAD AND CAKES

幸运饼干
xìngyùn bǐnggān
fortune cookies

白面包
báimiànbāo
white bread

黑面包
hēimiànbāo
brown bread

面包卷
miànbāojuǎn
roll

一块蛋糕
yīkuàidàngāo
slice of cake

饼干
bǐnggān
cookies

米饼
mǐbǐng
rice cakes

松饼
sōngbǐng
muffins

月饼
yuèbǐng
mooncakes

煎饼
jiānbǐng
pancakes

DAIRY PRODUCE

牛奶
niúnǎi
milk

豆奶
dòunǎi
soy milk

椰奶
yēnǎi
coconut milk

羊奶
yángnǎi
goat's milk

奶油
nǎiyóu
cream

生奶油
shēngnǎiyóu
whipped cream

奶酪
nǎilào
cheese

奶油干酪
nǎiyóugānlào
cream cheese

酸奶
suānnǎi
yogurt

冰激凌
bīngjīlíng
ice cream

NEWSPAPERS AND MAGAZINES

Do you have...	你有...? *nǐyǒu...*
...any more postcards?	...更多明信片吗? *gèngduō míngxìnpiàn ma*
...any American newspapers?	...英文报纸吗? *yīngwén bàozhǐ ma*
...airmail stamps?	...航空邮票吗? *hángkōng yóupiào ma*
...a pack of envelopes?	...一包信封吗? *yìbāo xìnfēng ma*
...some adhesive tape?	...一些透明胶带吗? *yìxiē tòumíngjiāodài ma*

邮票
yóupiào
stamps

铅笔
qiānbǐ
pencil

明信片
míngxìnpiàn
postcard

钢笔
gāngbǐ
pen

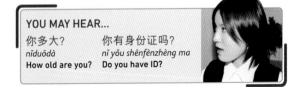

YOU MAY HEAR...

你多大?
nǐduōdà
How old are you?

你有身份证吗?
nǐ yǒu shēnfènzhèng ma
Do you have ID?

I'd like...　　　　　我想要...
　　　　　　　　　　wǒxiǎngyào

...a pack of cigarettes　...一盒烟
　　　　　　　　　　yīhéyān

...a box of matches　...一盒火柴
　　　　　　　　　　yīhé huǒchái

漫画
mànhuà
comic book

打火机
dǎhuǒjī
lighter

彩色铅笔
cǎisèqiānbǐ
colored pencils

口香糖
kǒuxiāngtáng
chewing gum

糖
táng
candy

烟丝
yānsī
tobacco

杂志
zázhì
magazine

报纸
bàozhǐ
newspaper

BUYING CLOTHES AND SHOES 🎧

I am looking for...	我在找... *wǒzàizhǎo*
I am size...	我穿...号 *wǒchuān ...hào*
Do you have this...	这个有... *zhègèyǒu*
...in my size?	...我的号吗? *wǒdehào ma*
...in small?	...小号吗? *xiǎohào ma*
...in medium?	...中号吗? *zhōnghào ma*
...in large?	...大号吗? *dàhào ma*
...in other colors?	...别的颜色吗? *biéde yánsè ma*
May I try this on?	我能试试吗? *wǒnéng shishi ma*
I'll take this one	我要这个 *wǒyào zhège*
It's...	这个... *zhège*
...too big	...太大 *tàidà*
...too small	...太小 *tàixiǎo*
I need...	我需要... *wǒxūyào*
...a larger size	...大一点的 *dàyīdiǎnde*
...a smaller size	...小一点的 *xiǎoyīdiǎnde*

I take shoe size...	我穿...号的鞋 wǒchuān ...hàodexié
May I try...	我能试... wǒnéngshì
...this pair?	...这双吗? zhèshuāngma
...those in the window?	...橱窗里的那双吗? chúchuānglǐde nàshuāngma
Is there a bigger size?	有大一号的吗? yǒu dàyīhàode ma
Is there a smaller size?	...有小一号的吗? yǒu xiǎoyīhàode ma
These are...	这些... zhèxiē
...too tight	...太挤 tàijǐ
...too small	...太小 tàixiǎo
...too big	...太大 tàidà
...uncomfortable	...不舒服 bùshūfu

CLOTHES SIZES GUIDE

Women's clothes	China	160–165	165–170	167–172	168–173	170–176
	US	2	4–6	8–10	12–14	16–18

Men's clothes	China	165	170	175	180	185
	International	S	M	L	XL	XXL

CLOTHES AND SHOES

连衣裙
liányīqún
dress

晚装
wǎnzhuāng
evening dress

夹克
jiákè
jacket

毛衣
máoyī
sweater

牛仔裤
niúzǎikù
jeans

裙子
qúnzi
skirt

运动鞋
yùndòngxié
sneakers

靴子
xuēzi
boots

手袋
shǒudài
handbag

皮带
pídài
belt

西装
xīzhuāng
suit

大衣
dàyī
coat

衬衫
chènshān
shirt

T恤衫
T xùshān
T-shirt

短裤
duǎnkù
shorts

高跟鞋
gāogēnxié
high-heeled shoes

系带鞋
jìdàixié
tie shoes

凉鞋
liángxié
sandals

平底人字拖鞋
píngdǐ rénzì tuōxié
flip-flops

袜子
wàzi
socks

AT THE GIFT SHOP

I'd like to buy a gift for...	我想给...买一个礼物 *wǒxiǎnggěi ...mǎi yīgè lǐwù*
...my mother/father	...我妈妈/爸爸 *wǒmāma / bàba*
...my daughter/son	...我女儿/儿子 *wǒnǚér / érzi*
...a child	...孩子 *háizi*
...a friend	...朋友 *péngyou*
Can you recommend something?	可以给我点建议吗? *kěyǐ gěiwǒdiǎn jiànyì ma*
Do you have a box for it?	有盒子吗? *yǒu hézi ma*
Can you gift-wrap it?	可以包成礼品吗? *kěyǐ bāochéng lǐpǐn ma*
Do you sell wrapping paper?	你们出售包装纸吗? *nǐmen chūshòu bāozhuāngzhǐ ma*

手链
shǒuliàn
bracelet

袖扣
xiùkòu
cufflinks

项链
xiàngliàn
necklace

手表
shǒubiǎo
watch

钱包
qiánbāo
wallet

娃娃
wáwa
doll

毛绒玩具
máoróng wánjù
stuffed animal

茶叶
cháyè
tea

I want a souvenir of...	我想要...的纪念品 *wǒxiǎngyào ...dejìniànpǐn*
Is there a guarantee?	有没有保修? *yǒuméiyǒu bǎoxiū*
May I exchange this?	我可以退换吗? *wǒkěyǐ tuìhuàn ma*
Here is the proof of the purchase	这是收据 *zhèshì shōujù*

YOU MAY HEAR...

这是作为礼品吗?
zhèshì zuòwéi lǐpǐn ma
Is it for a present?

帮你包成礼品吗?
bāngnǐ bāochénglǐpǐn ma
Shall I gift-wrap it?

PHOTOGRAPHY

I'd like this film developed	我想洗相片 *wǒxiǎng xǐ xiàngpiàn*
When will it be ready?	什么时候好? *shénmeshíhòu hǎo*
Do you have an express service?	你们有快速洗相服务吗? *nǐmen yǒu kuàisù xǐxiàng fúwù ma*
I'd like...	我想要... *wǒxiǎngyào*
...the one-hour service	...一小时洗相服务 *yīxiǎoshí xǐxiàngfúwù*
...a battery	...一块电池 *yīkuài diànchí*
...a disposable camera	...一次性相机 *yīcìxìng xiàngjī*

数码相机
shùmǎ xiàngjī
digital camera

记忆卡
jìyìkǎ
memory card

相框
xiàngkuàng
photo frame

相册
xiàngcè
photo album

Can you print from this
memory stick?

可以洗这个记忆卡里的相片吗？
kěyǐ xǐ zhège jìyìkǎlǐ de xiàngpiàn ma

My camera isn't working

我的相机坏了
wǒde xiàngjī huàile

镜头
jìngtóu
lens

照相机
zhàoxiàngjī
camera

相机包
xiàngjībāo
camera bag

闪光灯
shǎnguāngdēng
flash gun

YOU MAY HEAR...

要洗多大的？
yàoxǐ duōdàde
What size prints do you want?

无光泽/ 有光泽
wúguāngzé / yǒuguāngzé
matte/gloss

你什么时候要？
nǐ shénmeshíhòu yào
When do you want them?

AT THE POST OFFICE

I'd like...
我想要...
wǒxiǎngyào

...three stamps, please
...三张邮票
sānzhāng yóupiào

...to send this airmail
...发这封航空邮件
fā zhèfēng hángkōng yóujiàn

May I have a receipt, please?
请给我一个收据
qǐng gěiwǒ yīgè shōujù

邮票
yóupiào
stamps

信封
xìnfēng
envelope

航空邮件
hángkōngyóujiàn
airmail

明信片
míngxìnpiàn
postcard

YOU MAY HEAR...

里面是什么东西
lǐmiàn shì shénmedōngxī
What are the contents?

价值多少?
jiàzhí duōshǎo
What is their value?

填这张表
tián zhèzhāng biǎo
Fill out this form

How much is...	...多少钱
	duōshǎoqián
...a letter to...	...往...寄信
	wǎng ...jìxìn
...a postcard to...	...往...寄明信片
	wǎng ...jìmíngxìnpiàn
...the United States?	...美国?
	měiguó
...Great Britain?	...英国?
	yīngguó
...Canada?	...加拿大?
	jiānádà
...Australia?	...澳大利亚?
	àodàlìyà
Where can I mail this?	哪里可以寄这个?
	nǎlǐ kěyǐ jìzhège
Is there a mailbox?	这里有邮筒吗?
	zhèlǐ yǒu yóutǒng ma

包裹
bāoguǒ
package

速递
sùdì
courier

邮筒
yóutǒng
mailbox

邮递员
yóudìyuán
letter carrier

TELEPHONES

Where is the nearest phone shop?	最近的手机店在哪儿? *zuìjìnde shǒujīdiàn zàinǎr*
I'd like to make a collect call	我想打一个对方付费电话 *wǒxiǎng dǎyīgè duìfāng fùfèi diànhuà*
Who's speaking?	请问是哪位? *qǐngwèn shì nǎwèi*
Hello, this is...	喂，我是… *wéi, wǒshì*
I'd like to speak to...	我找… *wǒzhǎo*
May I leave a message?	我可以留言吗? *wǒ kěyǐ liúyán ma*

无绳电话
wúshéngdiànhuà
cordless phone

智能手机
zhìnéngshǒujī
smartphone

答录机
dálùjī
answering machine

手机
shǒujī
cell phone

投币电话
tóubì diànhuà
coin-operated phone

INTERNET

Is there an internet café near here?
这附近有网吧吗？
zhèfùjìn yǒu wǎngbā ma

How much do you charge?
怎么收费？
zěnme shōufèi

Do you have wireless internet?
有无线上网吗？
yǒu wúxiànshàngwǎng ma

May I check my emails?
可以查我的电子邮件吗？
kěyǐ chá wǒde diànzǐyóujiàn ma

I need to send an email
我想发一个电子邮件
wǒxiǎng fāyīgè diànzǐyóujiàn

What's your email address?
你的电子邮件地址是什么？
nǐde diànzǐyóujiàn dìzhǐ shìshénme

My email address is...
我的电子邮件地址是…
wǒde diànzǐyóujiàn dìzhǐ shì

May I send an email from here?
我可以从这儿发电子邮件吗？
wǒkěyǐ cóngzhèr fā diànzǐyóujiàn ma

手提电脑
shǒutídiànnǎo
laptop

键盘
jiànpán
keyboard

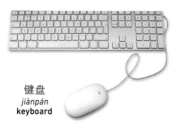

网站
wǎngzhàn
website

电子邮件
diànzǐyóujiàn
email

SIGHTSEEING

For the traveler, there is so much to see in a vast
country like China, ranging from city museums
and temples to the famous tourist sights, such as
the Great Wall of China. Most museums are open
all day from 8am onwards, although some close
for lunch. Virtually no sights are free and you will
have to pay an admission fee to enter most
temples, museums, parks, and wildlife reserves.

Can you recommend...	你能推荐...	*nǐ néng tuījiàn*
...a guided tour?	...一个导游带队游吗?	*yīgè dǎoyóudàiduì yóu ma*
...an excursion?	...一个短途旅行吗?	*yīgè duǎntú lǚxíng ma ?*
Is there a museum?	这儿有博物馆吗?	*zhèr yǒu bówùguǎn ma*
Is it open to the public?	向公众开放吗?	*xiàng gōngzhòngkāifàng ma*
Is there wheelchair access?	这儿有轮椅通道吗?	*zhèr yǒu lúnyǐtōngdào ma*
Does it close...	...关门吗	*guānménma*
...on Sundays?	周日...?	*zhōurì*
...on public holidays?	节假日...?	*jiéjiàrì*
How long does it take to get there?	去那儿要多长时间?	*qù nàr yào duōchángshíjiān*
Do you have...	你有...	*nǐyǒu*
...a street map?	...街道地图吗?	*jiēdàodìtú ma*
...a guide?	...指南吗?	*zhǐnán ma*
...any leaflets?	...宣传页吗?	*xuānchuányè ma*
Can you show me on the map?	你可以在地图上指给我看吗?	*nǐ kěyǐ zàidìtúshàng zhǐgěiwǒ kàn ma*

VISITING PLACES

What time...	你们什么时间... *nǐmen shénmeshíjiān*
...do you open?	...开门? *kāimén*
...do you close?	...关门? *guānmén*
I'd like two entrance tickets	我想要两张门票 *wǒ xiǎngyào liǎngzhāng ménpiào*
Two adults, please	请给我两张成人票 *qǐng gěiwǒ liǎngzhāng chéngrénpiào*
A family ticket	一张家庭票 *yīzhāng jiātíngpiào*
How much does it cost?	多少钱? *duōshǎo qián*
Are there reductions...	对...有优惠吗? *duì ...yǒu yōuhuì ma*
...for children?	...儿童 *értóng*
...for students?	...学生 *xuéshēng*
...for senior citizens?	...老年人 *lǎoniánrén*
...for disabled people?	...残疾人 *cánjírén*

地图
dìtú
map

街道地图
jiēdào dìtú
street map

门票
ménpiào
entrance ticket

轮椅通道
lúnyǐtōngdào
wheelchair access

Can I buy a guidebook?	我可以买一本旅行指南吗? *wǒ kěyǐ mǎi yīběn lǚxíng zhǐnán ma*
Is there...	这儿有... *zhèr yǒu*
...an audio guide?	...语音导览吗? *yǔyīndǎolǎn ma*
...a guided tour?	...导游带队游吗? *dǎoyóudàiduìyóu ma*
...an elevator?	...电梯吗? *diàntī ma*
...a café?	...咖啡馆吗? *kāfēiguǎn ma*
...a bus tour?	...巴士观光吗? *bāshìguānguāng ma*
When is the next tour?	下次游览什么时候? *xiàcì yóulǎn shénmeshíhòu*

观光巴士
guānguāngbāshì
tour bus

YOU MAY HEAR...

| 你多大了?
nǐ duōdà le
How old are you? | 你有学生证吗?
nǐ yǒu xuéshēngzhèng ma
Do you have a student ID? |

FINDING YOUR WAY

Excuse me
抱歉/打扰一下
bàoqiàn / dǎrǎoyīxià

Can you help me?
你能帮帮我吗？
nǐ néng bāngbang wǒ ma

Is this the way to...
这是去...的路吗
zhèshì qù ...de lù ma

How do I get to...
我怎么去...
wǒ zěnme qù

...the town center?
...市中心？
shìzhōngxīn

...the station?
...车站？
chēzhàn

...the museum?
...博物馆？
...bówùguǎn

...the art gallery?
...艺术馆？
yìshùguǎn

How long does it take?
需要多久
xūyào duōjiǔ

Is it far?
远吗？
yuǎn ma

Is it within walking distance?
是可以步行去的距离吗？
shì kěyǐ bùxíng qùdejùlí ma

Can you show me on the map?
你可以在地图上指给我看吗？
nǐ kěyǐ zàidìtúshàng zhǐgěiwǒ kàn ma

YOU MAY HEAR...

那不远
nà bù yuǎn
It's not far away

要10分钟
yào shí fēnzhōng
It takes ten minutes

YOU MAY HEAR...

我们在这儿
wǒmen zàizhèr
We are here

一直直走...
yīzhí zhízǒu
Keep going straight...

...到街的尽头
dào jiēdejìntóu
...to the end of the street

...到交通信号灯
dào jiāotōngxìnhàodēng
...to the traffic lights

...到主广场
dào zhǔguǎngchǎng
...to the main square

...这边走
zhèbiān zǒu
This way

...那边走
nàbiān zǒu
That way

在...向右拐
zài ...xiàngyòuguǎi
Turn right at...

在...向左拐
zài ...xiàngzuǒguǎi
Turn left at...

在第一个...
zài dìyīgè
Take the first...

...在左边/右边
zài zuǒbiān/yòubiān
...on the left/right

在你前面
zài nǐ qiánmiàn
It's in front of you

在你后面
zài nǐ hòumiàn
It's behind you

在你对面
zài nǐ duìmiàn
It's opposite you

在...旁边
zài ...pángbiān
It's next to...

有标识
yǒubiāoshí
It's signed

在那儿
zài nàr
It's over there

你需要乘坐公共汽车
nǐ xūyào chéngzuò gōnggòngqìchē
You need to take a bus

PLACES TO VISIT

市政厅
shìzhèngtīng
town hall

桥
qiáo
bridge

博物馆
bówùguǎn
museum

艺术馆
yìshùguǎn
art gallery

纪念碑
jìniànbēi
monument

塔
tǎ
pagoda

园林
yuánlín
gardens

寺庙
sìmiào
temple

公园
gōngyuán
park

节日
jiérì
festival

河流
héliú
river

村庄
cūnzhuāng
village

湖
hú
lake

海岸
hǎiàn
coast

瀑布
pùbù
waterfall

山脉
shānmài
mountains

OUTDOOR ACTIVITIES

Where can we go...
我们能去哪儿...
wǒmen néng qùnǎr

...cycling?
...骑自行车?
qí zìxíngchē

...fishing?
...钓鱼?
diàoyú

...swimming?
...游泳?
yóuyǒng

...walking?
...散步?
sànbù

...birdwatching?
...观鸟?
guānniǎo

...train spotting?
...猜火车?
cāihuǒchē

Can we...
我们可以...
wǒmen kěyǐ

...rent equipment?
...租设备吗?
zū shèbèi ma

...take lessons?
...上课吗?
shàngkè ma

How much per hour?
每小时多少钱?
měi xiǎoshí duōshǎo qián

I'm a beginner
我是初学者
wǒshì chūxuézhě

I'm very experienced
我相当有经验
wǒ xiāngdāng yǒujīngyàn

Is there a playground?
这儿有游乐场吗?
zhèr yǒu yóulèchǎng ma

Is it safe for children?
这对儿童安全吗?
zhè duì értóng ānquán ma

动物园
dòngwùyuán
zoo

游乐场
yóulèchǎng
playground

野餐
yěcān
picnic

骑自行车
qí zìxíngchē
cycling

钓鱼
diàoyú
fishing

骑马
qímǎ
horseback riding

攀岩
pānyán
climbing

观鸟
guānniǎo
birdwatching

SPORTS AND LEISURE

China can offer the traveler a wide range of cultural events, entertainment, leisure activities, and sports. Although theater and opera appeal only to a minority, most people enjoy going to the cinema and karaoke bars, and watching or playing sports. In addition to traditional pursuits, such as martial arts, wrestling, and kite flying, games such as table tennis, badminton, basketball, and soccer are increasingly popular, and you can even go skiing in the northeast of the country.

LEISURE TIME

I like...	我喜欢... *wǒ xǐhuān*
...art and painting	...艺术和绘画 *yìshù hé huìhuà*
...movies and film	...电影和电影院 *diànyǐng hé diànyǐngyuàn*
...the theater	...剧院 *jùyuàn*
...opera	...歌剧 *gējù*
I prefer...	我更喜欢... *wǒ gèng xǐhuān*
...reading books	...看书 *kànshū*
...listening to music	...听音乐 *tīng yīnyuè*
...watching sports	...看体育比赛 *kàn tǐyùbǐsài*
...going to concerts	...去听音乐会 *qùtīng yīnyuèhuì*
...dancing	...跳舞 *tiàowǔ*
...going to clubs	...去夜总会 *qù yèzǒnghuì*
...going out with friends	...和朋友出去 *hé péngyou chūqù*
I don't like...	我不喜欢... *wǒ bùxǐhuān*
That doesn't interest me	我对那个没兴趣 *wǒ duì nàge méixìngqù*

AT THE BEACH

Can I rent...
我可以租一个...
wǒ kěyǐ zūyīgè

...a jet ski?
...水上摩托吗?
shuǐshàngmótuō ma

...a beach umbrella?
...遮阳伞吗?
zhēyángsǎn ma

...a surfboard?
...冲浪板吗?
chōnglàngbǎn ma

...a wetsuit?
...潜水服吗?
qiánshuǐfú ma

海滩浴巾
hǎitānyùjīn
beach towel

轻便折叠躺椅
qīngbiàn shédié tǎngyǐ
deck chair

沙滩球
shātānqiú
beach ball

日光浴躺椅
rìguāngyùtǎngyǐ
lounge chair

YOU MAY HEAR...

禁止游泳
jìnzhǐ yóuyǒng
No swimming

海滩关闭
hǎitān guānbì
Beach closed

强流
qiángliú
Strong currents

How much does it cost?	多少钱? *duōshǎoqián*
Can I go water-skiing?	我可以去滑水吗? *wǒ kěyǐ qù huáshuǐ ma*
Is there a lifeguard?	这儿有救生员吗? *zhèr yǒu jiùshēngyuán ma*
Is it safe to...	...安全吗? *ānquán ma*
...swim here?	在这儿游泳... *zài zhèr yóuyǒng*
...surf here?	在这儿冲浪... *zài zhèr chōnglàng*

太阳镜
tàiyángjìng
sunglasses

遮阳帽
zhēyángmào
sun hat

脚蹼
jiǎopǔ
fins

防晒油
fángshàiyóu
suntan lotion

比基尼
bǐ jī ní
bikini

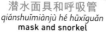

潜水面具和呼吸管
qiánshuǐmiànjù hé hūxīguǎn
mask and snorkel

AT THE SWIMMING POOL 🎧

What time...	什么时候... *shénmeshíhòu*
...does the pool open?	...游泳池开门? *yóuyǒngchí kāimén*
...does the pool close?	...游泳池关门? *yóuyǒngchí guānmén*
Is it...	这是... *zhèshì*
...an indoor pool?	...室内游泳池吗? *shìnèi yóuyǒngchí ma*
...an outdoor pool?	...室外游泳池吗? *shìwài yóuyǒngchí ma*
Is there a children's pool?	这儿有儿童游泳池吗? *zhèr yǒu értóng yóuyǒngchí ma*
Where are the changing rooms?	更衣室在哪儿? *gèngyīshì zàinǎr*
Is it safe to dive?	潜水安全吗? *qiánshuǐ ānquán ma*

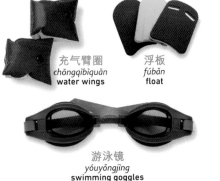

充气臂圈
chōngqìbìquān
water wings

浮板
fúbǎn
float

游泳镜
yóuyǒngjìng
swimming goggles

泳衣
yǒngyī
swimsuit

AT THE GYM

交叉训练器
jiāochā xùnliànqì
cross trainer

健身车
jiànshēnchē
exercise bike

划船机
huáchuánjī
rowing machine

踏步机
tàbùjī
step machine

Is there a gym?	这儿有健身房吗？ *zhèr yǒu jiànshēnfáng ma*
Is it free for guests?	这儿对客人免费吗？ *zhèr duì kèrén miǎnfèi ma*
Do I have to wear sneakers?	我必须穿运动鞋吗？ *wǒ bìxū chuān yùndòngxié ma*
Do I need an introductory session?	我需要上一个预备课吗？ *wǒ xūyào shàng yīgè yùbèikè ma*
Do you hold...	你们开办... *nǐmen kāibàn*
...aerobics classes?	...有氧运动课程吗？ *yǒuyǎngyùndòng kèchéng ma*
...Pilates classes?	...普拉提课程吗？ *pǔlātí kèchéng ma*
...yoga classes?	...瑜伽课程吗？ *yújiā kèchéng ma*

BOATING AND SAILING

Can I rent...
我可以租...
wǒkěyǐ zū

...a dinghy?
...一个橡皮艇吗?
yīgè xiàngpítǐng ma

...a windsurf board?
...一个帆板吗?
yīgè fānbǎn ma

...a canoe?
...独木舟吗?
dúmùzhōu ma

...a rowboat?
...划桨船吗?
huájiǎngchuán ma

Do you offer sailing lessons?
你们有帆船运动的课程吗?
nǐmen yǒu fānchuányùndòng de kèchéng ma

Do you have a mooring?
你们有停泊处吗?
nǐmen yǒu tíngbóchù ma

How much is it for the night?
一天多少钱?
yītiān duōshǎoqián

Can I buy gas?
我可以买燃气吗?
wǒ kěyǐ mǎi ránqì ma

Where is the marina?
小艇船坞在哪儿?
xiǎotǐng chuánwù zàinǎr

Can you repair it?
你可以修理它吗?
nǐkěyǐ xiūlǐtā ma

救生衣
jiùshēngyī
life jacket

指南针
zhǐnánzhēn
compass

WINTER SPORTS

I would like to rent...	我想租... *wǒxiǎngzū*
...some skis	...一些滑雪板 *yīxiē huáxuěbǎn*
...some ski boots	...一些滑雪靴 *yīxiē huáxuěxuē*
...some poles	...一些杆子 *yīxiē gānzi*
...a snowboard	...一个雪地滑板 *yīgè xuědìhuábǎn*
...a helmet	...一个头盔 *yīgè tóukuī*
When does...	什么时候... *shénmeshíhòu*
...the chair lift start?	...缆椅出发? *lǎnyǐ chūfā*
...the cable car finish?	...缆车服务结束? *lǎnchē fúwù jiéshù*
How much is a lift pass?	一个缆车套票多少钱? *yīgè lǎnchētàopiào duōshǎoqián*
Can I take skiing lessons?	我可以上滑雪课吗? *wǒkěyǐ shàng huáxuěkè ma*
Where are the green slopes?	练习坡地在哪儿? *liànxípōdì zàinǎr*

YOU MAY HEAR...

你是新手吗?
nǐ shì xīnshǒu ma
Are you a beginner?

需要押金
xūyào yājīn
I need a deposit

BALL GAMES

I like playing...	我喜欢玩... *wǒ xǐhuān wán*
...soccer	...足球 *zúqiú*
...tennis	...网球 *wǎngqiú*
...golf	...高尔夫 *gāoěrfū*
...badminton	...羽毛球 *yǔmáoqiú*
...squash	...壁球 *bìqiú*
...table tennis	...乒乓球 *pīngpāngqiú*
Where is...	...在哪儿 *zàinǎr*
...the tennis court?	网球场...? *wǎngqiúchǎng...*
...the golf course?	高尔夫球场...? *gāoěrfūqiúchǎng...*
...the sports center?	体育中心...? *tǐyùzhōngxīn...*

足球
zúqiú
soccer ball

球篮
qiúlán
basket

乒乓球拍
pīngpāngqiúpāi
table tennis bat

May I book a court...	我可以订一个球场... *wǒ kěyǐ dìng yīgè qiúchǎng*
...for two hours?	...打两个小时吗? *dǎ liǎnggè xiǎoshí ma*
...at three o'clock?	...3点开始打吗? *sāndiǎn kāishǐ dǎ ma*
What shoes are allowed?	允许穿哪些鞋? *yǔnxǔ chuān nǎxiēxié*
May I rent...	我可以租... *wǒkěyǐ zū*
...a tennis racket?	...一个网球拍吗? *yīgè wǎngqiúpāi ma*
...some balls?	...一些球吗? *yīxiē qiú ma*
...a set of clubs?	...一套球杆吗? *yītào qiúgān ma*
When is the game/match?	比赛在什么时候? *bǐsài zài shénme shíhòu*

网球
wǎngqiú
tennis balls

护腕
hùwàn
wristbands

网球拍
wǎngqiúpāi
tennis racket

高尔夫球杆
gāoěrfū qiúgān
golf club

高尔夫球和球座
gāoěrfūqiú hé qiúzuò
golf ball and tee

GOING OUT

Where is...	...在哪儿 *zài nǎr*
...the opera house?	歌剧院...? *gējùyuàn*
...the theater?	剧院...? *jùyuàn*
Do I have to book in advance?	我需要提前订票吗? *wǒxūyào tíqián dìngpiào ma*
I'd like...tickets	我想要...张票 *wǒxiǎngyào ...zhāngpiào*
I'd like seats...	我想要...的座位 *wǒxiǎngyào ...dezuòwèi*
...at the back	...在后面 *zài hòumiàn*
...at the front	...在前面 *zài qiánmiàn*
...in the middle	...在中间 *zài zhōngjiān*
...in the balcony	...在顶层 *zài dǐngcéng*
Is there live music?	这儿有现场音乐吗? *zhèr yǒu xiànchǎng yīnyuè ma*
Can we go dancing?	我们能去跳舞吗? *wǒmen néng qù tiàowǔ ma*

YOU MAY HEAR...

关掉你的移动电话
guāndiào nǐde
yídòngdiànhuà
Turn off your
cell phone

回到你的座位
huídào nǐde
zuòwèi
Return to your
seats

音乐家
yīnyuèjiā
musician

剧院
jùyuàn
theater

歌剧院
gējùyuàn
opera house

夜总会
yèzǒnghuì
nightclub

歌手
gēshǒu
singer

钢琴家
gāngqínjiā
pianist

电影院
diànyǐngyuàn
movie theater

爆米花
bàomǐhuā
popcorn

传统舞蹈家
chuántǒngwǔdǎojiā
traditional dancer

芭蕾舞
bālěiwǔ
ballet

GALLERIES AND MUSEUMS

What are the opening hours?	开放时间几点到几点？ *kāifàngshíjiān jǐdiǎn dào jǐdiǎn*
Are there guided tours in English?	有英文翻译的团体旅游吗？ *yǒu yīngwén fānyì de tuántǐlǚyóu ma*
When does the tour leave?	旅游团什么时候出发？ *lǚyóutuán shénmeshíhòu chūfā*
How much does it cost?	多少钱？ *duōshǎoqián*
How long does it take?	要多久？ *yàoduōjiǔ*
Do you have an audio guide?	有语音导游吗？ *yǒu yǔyīndǎoyóu ma*
Do you have a guidebook in English?	有英文的旅行指南吗？ *yǒu yīngwén de lǚxíngzhǐnán ma*
Is (flash) photography allowed?	允许照相吗？ *yǔnxǔ zhàoxiàng ma*
Can you direct me to...?	你能指给我怎么去...吗？ *nǐ néng zhǐgěiwǒ zěnmequ ...ma*

雕像
diāoxiàng
statue

半身像
bànshēnxiàng
bust

I'd really like to see...	我真的想看... *wǒ zhēnde xiǎngkàn*
Who painted this?	谁画的这幅画? *shuí huàde zhèfúhuà*
How old is it?	这个有多久的历史? *zhège yǒu duōjiǔ de lìshǐ*
Are there wheelchair ramps?	这儿有轮椅坡道吗? *zhèr yǒu lúnyǐ pōdào ma*
Is there an elevator?	这儿有电梯吗? *zhèr yǒu diàntī ma*
Where are the restrooms?	洗手间在哪儿? *xǐshǒujiān zài nǎr*
I'm with a group	我是跟团的 *wǒshì gēntuán de*
I've lost my group	我掉队了 *wǒ diàoduì le*

绘画
huìhuà
painting

素描
sùmiáo
drawing

版画
bǎnhuà
engraving

手稿
shǒugǎo
manuscript

HOME ENTERTAINMENT

How do I...	我怎么... *wǒzěnme*
...turn on the television?	...打开电视机? *dǎkāi diànshìjī*
...change channels?	...换频道? *huàn píndào*
...turn up the volume?	提高音量? *tígāo yīnliàng*
...turn down the volume?	降低音量? *jiàngdī yīnliàng*
Do you have satellite TV?	有卫星电视吗? *yǒu wèixīngdiànshì ma*
Can I access English language channels?	可以收到英语频道吗? *kěyǐ shōudào yīngyǔpíndào ma*
Where can I buy...	在哪儿能买到... *zàinǎr néng mǎidào*
...a music CD?	...音乐CD? *yīnyuè CD*
...an audio CD?	...音频CD? *yīnpín CD*

DVD播放器
DVD bōfàngqì
DVD player

宽屏电视
kuānpíngdiànshì
widescreen TV

遥控器
yáokòngqì
remote control

电子游戏
diànzǐ yóuxì
video game

U盘
U pán
USB flash drive

笔记本电脑
bǐjìběn diànnǎo
laptop

收音机
shōuyīnjī
radio

硬盘
yìngpán
hard drive

鼠标
shǔbiāo
mouse

Can I use this to...	我可以用这个... *wǒ kěyǐ yòng zhège*
...go online?	...上网吗? *shàngwǎng ma*
Is it broadband/wifi?	这是宽带/无线网络吗? *zhèshì kuāndài / wúxiànwǎngluò ma*
How do I...	我怎么... *wǒzěnme*
...log on?	...登录? *dēnglù*
...log out?	...退出? *tuìchū*
...reboot?	...重新启动? *chóngxīn qǐdòng*

HEALTH

Unlike in the United States, most Chinese doctors are based in hospitals; you will need to make an appointment to see one. Many pharmacies stock Western medicines as well as traditional Chinese remedies and can treat you for most minor health problems. It is a good idea to familiarize yourself with a few basic phrases for use in an emergency or in case you need to visit a pharmacy or doctor.

USEFUL PHRASES

| I need a doctor | 我需要看医生 |
| | *wǒ xūyào kànyīshēng* |

| I would like an appointment... | 我想预约... |
| | *wǒ xiǎng yùyuē* |

| ...as soon as possible | ...尽快 |
| | *jìnkuài* |

| ...today | ...今天 |
| | *jīntiān* |

| ...tomorrow | ...明天 |
| | *míngtiān* |

| It's very urgent | 这十分紧急 |
| | *zhè shífèn jǐnjí* |

| I have health insurance | 我有健康保险 |
| | *wǒ yǒu jiànkāngbǎoxiǎn* |

| May I have a receipt? | 可以给我一个收据吗? |
| | *kěyǐ gěiwǒ yīgè shōujù ma* |

| Where is the nearest... | 附近哪儿有... |
| | *fùjìn nǎryǒu* |

| ...pharmacy? | ...药房? |
| | *yàofáng* |

| ...doctor's office? | ...诊所? |
| | *zhěnsuǒ* |

| ...hospital? | ...医院? |
| | *yīyuàn* |

| ...dentist? | ...牙医? |
| | *yáyī* |

| What are the opening times? | 开门时间几点到几点? |
| | *kāiménshíjiān jǐdiǎn dào jǐdiǎn* |

| I need a dentist | 我需要看牙医 |
| | *wǒ xūyào kànyáyī* |

AT THE PHARMACY

What can I take for...?	治...应当服什么药？ *zhì ...yīngdāng fú shénmeyào*
How much should I take?	应当服多少？ *yīngdāng fú duōshǎo*
Is it safe for children?	这对儿童安全吗？ *zhè duì értóng ānquán ma*
Are there side effects?	有副作用吗？ *yǒu fùzuòyòng ma*
Do you have that...	这种药有... *zhèzhǒngyào yǒu*
...in tablet form?	...药片的吗？ *yàopiàn de ma*
...as a syrup?	...糖浆的吗？ *tángjiāng de ma*
...in capsule form?	...胶囊的吗？ *jiāonáng de ma*
I'm allergic to...	我对...过敏 *wǒduì ...guòmǐn*
I'm already taking...	我已经在吃... *wǒ yǐjīng zàichī*
Do I need a prescription?	我需要一个处方吗？ *wǒ xūyào yīgèchǔfāng ma*

YOU MAY HEAR...

这个一天吃...次
zhège yītiān chī... cì
Take this...times a day

怎么了？ *zěnmele* **What's the matter?**	随餐服用 *suícān fúyòng* **With food**

全国药品零售企业统一标志

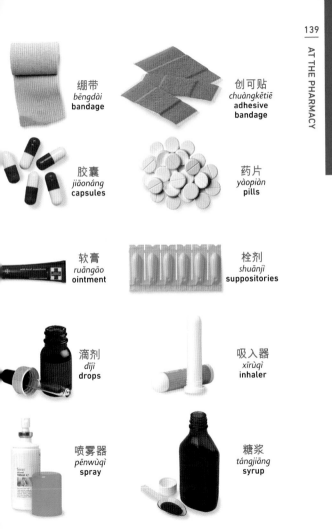

绷带
bēngdài
bandage

创可贴
chuàngkětiē
adhesive
bandage

胶囊
jiāonáng
capsules

药片
yàopiàn
pills

软膏
ruǎngāo
ointment

栓剂
shuānjì
suppositories

滴剂
dījì
drops

吸入器
xīrùqì
inhaler

喷雾器
pēnwùqì
spray

糖浆
tángjiāng
syrup

THE HUMAN BODY

I have hurt my...   我伤到了我的...
wǒ shāngdàole wǒde

I have cut my...   我割伤了我的...
wǒ gēshāngle wǒde

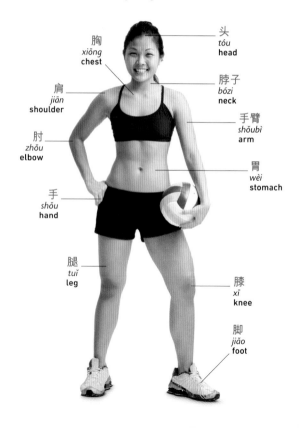

胸
xiōng
chest

头
tóu
head

肩
jiān
shoulder

脖子
bózi
neck

肘
zhǒu
elbow

手臂
shǒubì
arm

手
shǒu
hand

胃
wèi
stomach

腿
tuǐ
leg

膝
xī
knee

脚
jiǎo
foot

FACE

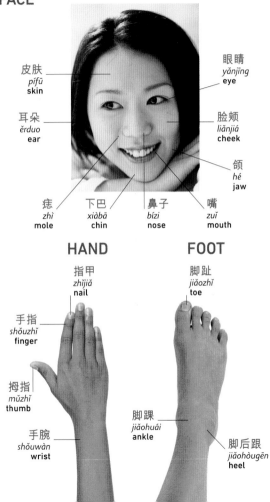

皮肤
pífū
skin

眼睛
yǎnjīng
eye

耳朵
ěrduo
ear

脸颊
liǎnjiá
cheek

颌
hé
jaw

痣
zhì
mole

下巴
xiàbā
chin

鼻子
bízi
nose

嘴
zuǐ
mouth

HAND

FOOT

指甲
zhǐjiǎ
nail

脚趾
jiǎozhǐ
toe

手指
shǒuzhǐ
finger

拇指
mǔzhǐ
thumb

手腕
shǒuwàn
wrist

脚踝
jiǎohuái
ankle

脚后跟
jiǎohòugēn
heel

FEELING SICK 🎧

I don't feel well	我不舒服 *wǒ bù shūfu*
I feel sick	我病了 *wǒ bìng le*
I have...	我... *wǒ*
...an ear ache	...耳痛 *ěrtòng*
...a stomach ache	...胃痛 *wèitòng*
...a sore throat	...嗓子痛 *sǎngzitòng*
...a temperature	...发烧了 *fāshāole*
...hayfever	...枯草热 *kūcǎorè*
...constipation	...便秘 *biànmì*
...diarrhea	...腹泻 *fùxiè*
...toothache	...牙痛 *yátòng*
I've been stung/bitten by...	我被...叮/咬了 *wǒbèi ...dīng / yǎo le*
...a bee/wasp	蜜蜂/黄蜂 *mìfēng / huángfēng*
...a jellyfish	水母 *shuǐmǔ*
...a snake	蛇 *shé*
I've been bitten by a dog	我被狗咬了 *wǒ bèi gǒu yǎo le*

INJURIES

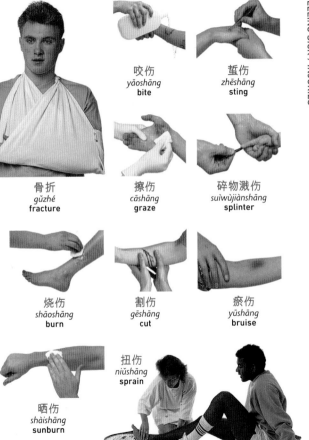

咬伤
yǎoshāng
bite

蜇伤
zhēshāng
sting

骨折
gǔzhé
fracture

擦伤
cāshāng
graze

碎物溅伤
suìwùjiànshāng
splinter

烧伤
shāoshāng
burn

割伤
gēshāng
cut

瘀伤
yūshāng
bruise

晒伤
shàishāng
sunburn

扭伤
niǔshāng
sprain

AT THE DOCTOR

I need to see a doctor	我需要看医生
	wǒ xūyào kànyīshēng
It hurts here	这里痛
	zhèlǐ tòng
I'm...	我
	wǒ
...vomiting	...呕吐
	ǒutù
...bleeding	...流血
	liúxiě
...feeling faint	...头晕
	tóuyūn
I'm pregnant	我怀孕了
	wǒ huáiyùn le
I'm diabetic	我是糖尿病患者
	wǒshì tángniàobìng huànzhě
I'm epileptic	我是癫痫患者
	wǒshì diānxián huànzhě
I have...	我有...
	wǒ yǒu
...arthritis	...关节炎
	guānjiéyán
...a heart condition	...心脏病
	xīnzàngbìng

YOU MAY HEAR...

怎么了?	哪里痛?	我可以给你做个检查吗?
zěnme le	*nǎlǐ tòng*	*wǒ kěyǐ gěinǐ zuògè jiǎnchá ma*
What's wrong?	**Where does it hurt?**	**May I examine you?**

ILLNESS

咳嗽
késòu
cough

哮喘
xiāochuǎn
asthma

感冒
gǎnmào
cold

流感
liúgǎn
the flu

喷嚏
pēntì
sneeze

痉挛
jìngluán
cramps

恶心
ěxin
nausea

皮疹
pízhěn
rash

鼻出血
bíchūxiě
nosebleed

头痛
tóutòng
headache

AT THE HOSPITAL

Can you help me?	可以帮帮我吗？ kěyǐ bāngbang wǒ ma
I need	我需要... wǒ xūyào
...a doctor	...一个医生 yīgè yīshēng
...a nurse	...一个护士 yīgè hùshì
Where is/are...	哪里是... nǎlǐ shì
...the emergency room?	...急诊处？ jízhěnchù
...the children's ward?	...儿童病房？ értóng bìngfáng
...the X-ray department?	...X光部门？ X guāng bùmén
...the waiting room?	...候诊室？ hòuzhěnshì

注射
zhùshè
injection

X光
X guāng
X-ray

验血
yànxiě
blood test

CT扫描
CT sǎomiáo
CT scan

...the intensive care unit?   ...重症监护室?
zhòngzhèngjiānhùshì

...the elevator/stairs?   ...电梯/楼梯?
diàntī / lóutī

I've broken...   我伤了...
wǒshāngle...

Do I need...   我需要...
wǒ xūyào

...an injection?   ...注射吗?
zhùshè ma

...antibiotics?   ...打抗生素吗?
dǎ kàngshēngsù ma

...an operation?   ...动手术吗?
dòng shǒushù ma

Will it hurt?   会痛吗?
huì tòng ma

What are the visiting hours?   探视时间是什么时候?
tànshìshíjiān shì shénmeshíhòu

Am I going to be all right?   我会好起来吗?
wǒ huì hǎoqǐlái ma

轮椅
lúnyǐ
wheelchair

复苏术
fùsūshù
resuscitation

医用夹板
yīyòngjiábǎn
splint

包扎
bāozhā
dressing

EMERGENCIES

In the event of an emergency, you should dial one of the following emergency numbers: 110 for the police, 119 for the fire department, and 120 for an ambulance. If you are the victim of a crime or you lose your passport and money, you should report the incident to the police, although it may be best to seek advice first from your local embassy or consulate staff, who will be able to help you.

IN AN EMERGENCY

Help!	救命! *jiùmìng*
Please go away!	请走开! *qǐngzǒukāi*
Let go!	放手! *fàngshǒu*
Stop! Thief!	站住! 小偷! *zhànzhù ! xiǎotōu!*
Call the police!	打电话叫警察! *dǎdiànhuà jiàojǐngchá*
Get a doctor!	叫医生! *jiào yīshēng*
I need...	我需要... *wǒxūyào*
...the police	...叫警察 *jiào jǐngchá*
...the fire department	...消防队 *xiāofángduì*
...an ambulance	...救护车 *jiùhùchē*
It's very urgent	非常紧急 *fēichángjǐnjí*
Where is...	...在哪里? *...zàinǎlǐ*
...the American/British embassy?	美国大使馆 / 英国大使馆...? *měiguó dàshǐguǎn/yīngguó dàshǐguǎn...*
...the American/British consulate?	美国领事馆 / 英国领事馆...? *měiguó lǐngshìguǎn/yīngguó lǐngshìguǎn...*
...the police station?	警察局...? *jǐngchájú...*
...the hospital?	医院...? *yīyuàn...*

ACCIDENTS

I need to make a telephone call	我需要打个电话 wǒ xūyào dǎgè diànhuà
I'd like to report an accident	我要报告一起事故 wǒ yào bàogào yīqǐshìgù
I've crashed my car	我撞车了 wǒ zhuàngchē le
The registration number is...	登记号码是... dēngjì hàomǎ shì
I'm at...	我在... wǒzài
Please come quickly!	请快来! qǐngkuàilái
Someone's injured	有人受伤了 yǒurén shòushāng le
Someone's been knocked down	有人被撞倒了 yǒurén bèi zhuàngdǎo le
There's a fire at...	...着火了 zháohuǒle
Someone is trapped in the building	有人被困在楼里了 yǒurén bèikùnzài lóulǐ le
My child is missing	我孩子不见了 wǒ háizi bújiàn le

YOU MAY HEAR...

你需要什么服务?
nǐ xūyào shénmefúwù
Which service do you require?

发生了什么事?
fāshēngle shénmeshì
What happened?

EMERGENCY SERVICES

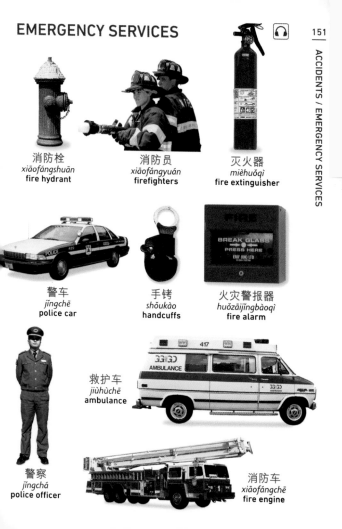

消防栓
xiāofángshuān
fire hydrant

消防员
xiāofángyuán
firefighters

灭火器
mièhuǒqì
fire extinguisher

警车
jǐngchē
police car

手铐
shǒukào
handcuffs

火灾警报器
huǒzāijǐngbàoqì
fire alarm

救护车
jiùhùchē
ambulance

警察
jǐngchá
police officer

消防车
xiāofángchē
fire engine

POLICE AND CRIME

I want to report a crime	我要报警 *wǒ yào bàojǐng*
I've been robbed	我被抢劫了 *wǒbèi qiǎngjié le*
I've been attacked	我被袭击了 *wǒbèi xíjī le*
I've been mugged	我遭暴力抢劫了 *wǒ zāo bàolìqiǎngjié le*
I've been raped	我被强奸了 *wǒbèi qiángjiān le*
I've been burgled	我被偷了 *wǒbèi tōule*
Someone has stolen...	有人偷了... *yǒurén tōule*
...my money	...我的钱 *wǒdeqián*
...my wallet	...我的钱包 *wǒde qiánbāo*
...my passport	...我的护照 *wǒde hùzhào*
...my handbag	...我的手提包 *wǒde shǒutíbāo*

YOU MAY HEAR...

什么时候发生的?
shénmeshíhòu fāshēng de
When did it happen?

他长什么样子?
tā zhǎng shénmeyàngzi
What did he look like?

有目击者么?
yǒu mùjīzhě ma
Was there a witness?

I'd like to speak to...	我找... *wǒzhǎo*
...a senior officer	...高级警官 *gāojí jǐngguān*
...a policewoman	...一位女警 *yīwèi nǚjǐng*
I need...	我需要... *wǒ xūyào*
...a lawyer	...一个律师 *yīgè lǜshī*
...an interpreter	...一个翻译 *yīgè fānyì*
...to make a phone call	...打个电话 *dǎgè diànhuà*
...a police report	...一份警方报告 *yīfèn jǐngfāng bàogào*
Here is...	这是... *zhèshì*
...my driver's license	...我的驾驶执照 *wǒde jiàshǐzhízhào*
...my insurance document	...我的保险证明 *wǒde bǎoxiǎnzhèngmíng*
How much is the fine?	罚款多少钱？ *fákuǎn duōshǎoqián*
Where do I pay it?	在哪儿交钱？ *zàinǎr jiāoqián*

YOU MAY HEAR...

请出示你的执照
qǐngchūshì nǐde zhízhào
Your license please

请出示你的文件
qǐngchūshì nǐde wénjiàn
Your papers please

AT THE GARAGE 🎧

Where is the nearest garage?	最近的汽车修理站在哪儿? zuìjìnde qìchēxiūlǐzhàn zàinǎr
Can you do repairs?	你做维修么? nǐ zuò wéixiū ma
I need...	我需要... wǒxūyào
...a new tire	...一个新轮胎 yīgè xīnlúntāi
...a new exhaust	...一个新的排气管 yīgè xīnde páiqìguǎn
...a new windshield	...一个新的风挡 yīgè xīnde fēngdǎng
...a new headlight	...一个新灯泡 yīgè xīndēngpào
...new wiper blades	...新的雨刷片 xīnde yǔshuāpiàn
Do you have one?	你有么? nǐyǒuma
Can you replace this?	你能帮我换掉这个吗? nǐnéng bāngwǒ huàndiào zhège ma
The...is not working	...坏了 huàile
There is something wrong with the engine	引擎有点问题 yǐnqíng yǒudiǎn wèntí
Is it serious?	严重吗? yánzhòng ma
When will it be ready?	什么时候能弄好? shénmeshíhòu néng nònghǎo
How much will it cost?	多少钱? duōshǎoqián

CAR BREAKDOWN

My car has broken down	我的车坏了 *wǒdechē huàile*
Can you help me?	你能帮我吗? *nǐ néng bāngwǒ ma*
Please come to...	请来... *qǐnglái*
I have a flat tire	我车胎被扎了 *wǒchētāi bèizhā le*
Can you change the wheel?	能帮我换车轮吗? *néng bāngwǒ huàn chēlún ma*
I need a new tire	我需要一个轮胎 *wǒ xūyào yīgè lúntāi*
My car won't start	我的车发动不起来 *wǒdechē fādòng bùqǐlái*
The engine is overheating	引擎过热了 *yǐnqíng guòrèle*
Can you fix it?	你能修好吗? *nǐnéng xiūhǎo ma*
I've run out of gasoline	车没油了 *chē méiyóu le*
Can you tow me to a garage?	你能把车拖到一个汽车修理站吗? *nǐnéng bǎchē tuōdào yīgè qìchēxiūlǐzhàn ma*

YOU MAY HEAR...

有什么问题?
yǒu shénmewèntí
What is the problem?

有备用轮胎吗?
yǒu bèiyònglúntāi ma
Do you have a spare tire?

LOST PROPERTY

I've lost...	我丢了... *wǒdiūle*
...my money	...我的钱 *wǒde qián*
...my keys	...我的钥匙 *wǒde yàoshi*
...my glasses	...我的眼镜 *wǒde yǎnjìng*
My luggage is missing	我的行李不见了 *wǒde xíngli bújiànle*
My suitcase has been damaged	我的箱子受损了 *wǒde xiāngzi shòusǔnle*
My bags have not arrived	我的包还没有到 *wǒdebāo háiméiyǒu dào*

钱夹
qiánjiā
wallet

护照
hùzhào
passport

信用卡
xìnyòngkǎ
credit card

钱包
qiánbāo
change purse

照相机
zhàoxiàngjī
camera

智能手机
zhìnéngshǒujī
smartphone

公文包
gōngwénbāo
briefcase

手提包
shǒutíbāo
handbag

箱子
xiāngxi
suitcase

I need to phone my insurance company	我需要给保险公司打电话 *wǒ xūyào gěi bǎoxiǎngōngsī dǎdiànhuà*
Can I put a stop on my credit cards?	我能终止我的信用卡吗？ *wǒ néng zhōngzhǐ wǒde xìnyòngkǎ ma*
My name is...	我叫... *wǒjiào*
My policy number is...	我的保险单号是... *wǒde bǎoxiǎndānhào shì*
My address is...	我的地址是... *wǒde dìzhǐshì*
My contact number is...	我的联系电话是... *wǒde liánxìdiànhuà shì*
My email address is...	我的电子邮件地址是... *wǒde diànzǐyóujiàndìzhǐ shì*

MENU GUIDE

This guide lists the most common terms that you may come across on Chinese menus. Dishes are divided into categories and the Chinese script is clearly displayed to help you identify the characters for particular items on a menu.

COOKING METHODS

barbecued...	烧烤...	shāokǎo...
diced...	块状...	kuàizhuàng...
curried...	咖喱...	gālí...
deep-fried...	炸...	zhá...
crispy deep-fried...	酥炸...	sūzhá...
stir-fried...	炒...	chǎo...
stir-fried...with sauce	酱炒...	jiàngchǎo...
quick-fried...	爆...	bào...
roasted...	烤...	kǎo...
...chunks, pieces	...段，块儿	...duàn, kuàir
stewed...	炖...	dùn...
...in hotpot	...火锅	...huǒguō
steamed...	清蒸...	qīngzhēng ...
home-style...	家常...	jiācháng ...
sliced...	片...	...piàn

"three-fresh"...	三鲜...	*sānxiān ...*
shredded...	...丝	*...sī*
stuffed...	包...	*bāo ...*
sweet and sour...balls	糖醋...丸	*tángcù ...wán*

BASIC FOODS

bread	面包	*miànbāo*
steamed rolls	蒸花卷	*zhēnghuājuǎn*
steamed bread	蒸馒头	*zhēngmántou*
cheese	奶酪	*nǎilào*
eggs	鸡蛋	*jīdàn*
meat	肉	*ròu*
pickles	咸菜	*xiáncài*
soy sauce	酱油	*jiàngyóu*
brown sauce	沙茶酱	*shāchájiàng*
chili sauce	辣椒酱	*làjiāojiàng*
Hoisin sauce	海鲜酱	*hǎixiānjiàng*
fish sauce	鱼酱	*yújiàng*
oyster sauce	蚝油	*háoyóu*
shrimp paste	虾酱	*xiājiàng*
black bean sauce	豆豉	*dòuchǐ*

yellow bean sauce	黄豆酱	*huángdòujiàng*
tomato sauce	番茄酱	*fānqiéjiàng*
vinegar	醋	*cù*
salt	盐	*yán*
pepper	柿子椒	*shìzǐjiāo*
peppercorns	花椒	*huājiāo*
sesame seeds	芝麻	*zhīmá*
peanuts	花生	*huāshēng*
sugar	糖	*táng*
artificial sweetener	人造糖	*rénzàotáng*
honey	蜂蜜	*fēngmì*
jam	果酱	*guǒjiàng*
cereal	谷物食品	*gǔwùshípǐn*
pancakes	煎饼	*jiānbǐng*

FIRST COURSES

spring rolls	春卷	*chūnjuǎn*
dumplings	饺子	*jiǎozi*
steamed dumplings	蒸饺	*zhēngjiǎo*
steamed dumplings with ground pork	猪肉馅蒸饺	*zhūròuxiàn zhēngjiǎo*
steamed dumplings with barbecued pork filling	叉烧馅蒸饺	*chāshāoxiàn zhēngjiǎo*
steamed meat buns	蒸肉包	*zhēngròubāo*
fried dumplings	煎饺	*jiānjiǎo*
deep-fried wontons	炸馄饨	*zháhúntun*
"seaweed"	"海带"	*"hǎidài "*
spiced spare ribs	五香排骨	*wǔxiāngpáigǔ*
chicken feet	凤爪	*fèngzhǎo*
stir-fried shrimp	炒虾仁	*chǎoxiārén*
deep-fried Phoenix-tail shrimp	炸凤尾虾	*zháfèngwěixiā*
shrimp wrapped in rice paper	纸包虾	*zhǐbāoxiā*
stuffed crab claws	蟹钳	*xièqián*
pickled vegetables	泡菜	*pàocài*

SOUPS

soup	汤	tāng
broth	肉汤	ròutāng
seaweed and dried prawn soup	虾干海带汤	xiāgānhǎidàitāng
"three-fresh" soup (normally prawn, meats, and vegetable)	三鲜汤	sānxiāntāng
soup with spinach and vermicelli	菠菜挂面汤	bōcàiguàmiàntāng
soup with eggs and tomato	番茄鸡蛋汤	fānqiéjīdàntāng
soup with sliced pork and vegetables	鲜肉时蔬汤	xiānròushíshūtāng
soup with shredded pork and pickled mustard greens	芥菜肉丝汤	jiècàiròusītāng
egg drop soup	鸡蛋汤	jīdàntāng
hot and sour soup	酸辣汤	suānlàtāng
bean curd soup	豆腐汤	dòufutāng
bird's nest soup	燕窝汤	yànwōtāng
wonton soup	馄饨汤	húntuntāng
shark's fin soup	鱼翅	yúchì
chicken soup	鸡汤	jītāng
vegetable soup	蔬菜汤	shūcàitāng
sweetcorn soup	玉米汤	yùmǐtāng
ginger soup with pork	姜片猪肉汤	jiāngpiànzhūròutāng
Cantonese fire pot	广式火锅	guǎngshìhuǒguō
Mongolian lamb	蒙古羊肉	ménggǔyángròu
fire pot	火锅	huǒguō

PORK

pork	猪肉	*zhūròu*
barbecued pork	烤猪肉	*kǎozhūròu*
sweet and sour pork	糖醋里脊	*tángcùlǐjǐ*
Cantonese roast pork	叉烧	*chāshāo*
steamed pork with rice	猪肉蒸饭	*zhūròuzhēngfàn*
stir-fried diced pork with chili	辣椒炒肉片	*làjiāochǎoròupiàn*
stir-fried sliced pork with bamboo shoots	竹笋炒肉片	*zhúsǔnchǎoròupiàn*
twice-cooked pork	回锅肉	*huíguōròu*
roast belly of pork	红烧猪肚	*hóngshāozhūdǔ*
spare ribs cooked in a sweet and sour sauce	糖醋排骨	*tángcùpáigǔ*
barbecued spare ribs	烤排骨	*kǎopáigǔ*
sausage	香肠	*xiāngcháng*
ham	火腿	*huǒtuǐ*
bacon	培根	*péigēn*

POULTRY

chicken	鸡肉	*jīròu*
diced chicken	鸡丁	*jīdīng*
stir-fried chicken	炒鸡肉	*chǎojīròu*
quick-fried diced chicken with bean sauce	酱爆鸡丁	*jiàngbàojīdīng*
"beggar's chicken" (charcoal-baked marinated chicken)	叫化鸡	*jiàohuājī*
Kung Pao chicken	宫保鸡丁	*gōngbǎojīdīng*
red-braised chicken	红烧鸡肉	*hóngshāojīròu*
soy sauce chicken	酱油鸡	*jiàngyóujī*
chicken livers	鸡肝	*jīgān*
sautéed chicken livers	嫩煎鸡肝	*nènjiānjīgān*
duck	鸭肉	*yāròu*
Peking roast duck	北京烤鸭	*běijīngkǎoyā*
duck's foot with mushroom	蘑菇鸭掌	*móguyāzhǎng*
smoked duck	熏鸭	*xūnyā*
stuffed duck	填鸭	*tiányā*
goose	鹅	*é*

BEEF AND LAMB

beef	牛肉	*niúròu*
quick-fried beef with Chinese onions	葱爆牛肉	*cōngbàoniúròu*
stir-fried beef with peanuts and chili	辣椒花生炒牛肉	*làjiāo huāshēng chǎo niúròu*
stir-fried beef in hot spicy sauce	香辣酱炒牛肉	*xiānglàjiàngchǎoniúròu*
beef braised in brown sauce	红烧牛肉	*hóngshāoniúròu*
green pepper beef in black bean sauce	青椒豆豉牛肉	*qīngjiāodòuchǐniúròu*
beef in oyster sauce	蚝油牛肉	*háoyóuniúròu*
steak	牛排	*niúpái*
veal	小牛肉	*xiǎoniúròu*
lamb	羊肉	*yángròu*
lamb kebabs	羊肉串	*yángròuchuàn*
Mongolian hotpot	蒙古火锅	*ménggǔhuǒguō*

OFFAL

heart	心	*xīn*
liver	肝	*gān*
kidneys	腰子	*yāozi*
ox tongue	牛舌	*niúshé*
tripe	牛肚	*niúdǔ*
entrails	肠子	*chángzi*

FISH AND SHELLFISH

fish	鱼肉	*yúròu*
seafood	海鲜	*hǎixiān*
shellfish	贝类	*bèilèi*
fish slices	鱼片	*yúpiàn*
sweet and sour fish	糖醋鱼	*tángcùyú*
stir-fried fish slices with thick sauce	酱炒鱼片	*jiàngchǎoyúpiàn*
prawns	虾	*xiā*
stir-fried prawns with egg white	滑蛋虾仁	*huádànxiārén*
stir-fried prawns in tomato sauce	番茄酱炒虾仁	*fānqiéjiàngchǎo xiārén*

spiced salt prawns	椒盐虾	*jiāoyánxiā*
shrimp	虾仁	*xiārén*
dried shrimp	海米	*hǎimǐ*
squid	鱿鱼	*yóuyú*
carp	鲤鱼	*lǐyú*
steamed carp	清蒸鲤鱼	*qīngzhēnglǐyú*
carp braised in brown sauce	红烧鲤鱼	*hóngshāolǐyú*
swordfish	剑鱼	*jiànyú*
scallops	扇贝	*shànbèi*
clams	蛤蜊	*gélí*
mussels	贻贝	*yíbèi*
crab	螃蟹	*pángxiè*
octopus	八爪鱼	*bāzhuǎyú*
oysters	牡蛎	*mǔlì*
sea bass	海鲈	*hǎilú*
abalone	鲍鱼	*bàoyú*
shark's fin	鱼翅	*yúchì*
eel	鳗鱼	*mányú*
eel braised with chili and bean sauce	豉椒烧鳗鱼	*chǐjiāoshāományú*

RICE AND NOODLES

noodles	面条	*miàntiáo*
rice noodles	米粉	*mǐfěn*
egg noodles	鸡蛋面	*jīdànmiàn*
cellophane noodles	粉丝	*fěnsī*
fried noodles	炒面	*chǎomiàn*
fried rice noodles	炒米粉	*chǎomǐfěn*
Singapore noodles	星洲炒米	*xīngzhōuchǎomǐ*
spicy Sichuan noodles	担担面	*dàndànmiàn*
rice	米饭	*mǐfàn*
glutinous rice	糯米	*nuòmǐ*
boiled rice	白饭	*báifàn*
stir-fried rice	炒饭	*chǎofàn*
plain fried rice	白炒饭	*báichǎofàn*
egg-fried rice	蛋炒饭	*dànchǎofàn*
special fried rice	特色炒饭	*tèsèchǎofàn*
sizzling rice	锅巴	*guōbā*
fried rice sticks	炒米线	*chǎomǐxiàn*
rice porridge	粥	*zhōu*

VEGETABLES, HERBS, AND SPICES

vegetables	蔬菜	*shūcài*
steamed vegetables	清蒸蔬菜	*qīngzhēngshūcài*
stir-fried seasonal vegetables	清炒时蔬	*qīngchǎoshíshū*
asparagus	芦笋	*lúsǔn*
beans	豆	*dòu*
green beans	绿豆	*lǜdòu*
soy beans	大豆	*dàdòu*
bean sprouts	豆芽	*dòuyá*
peas	豌豆	*wāndòu*
stir-fried peas with mushrooms	豌豆炒蘑菇	*wāndòuchǎomógu*
bok choy	小白菜	*xiǎobáicài*
broccoli	西兰花	*xīlánhuā*
cabbage	卷心菜	*juǎnxīncài*
Chinese cabbage	白菜	*báicài*
carrot	胡萝卜	*húluóbo*
spinach	菠菜	*bōcài*
cauliflower	花椰菜	*huāyēcài*
bamboo shoots	竹笋	*zhúsǔn*
mushrooms	蘑菇	*mógu*
onion	洋葱	*yángcōng*
scallions	葱	*cōng*
cucumber	黄瓜	*huángguā*
radish	萝卜	*luóbo*

red/green pepper	红/绿柿子椒	*hóng / lù shìzijiāo*
corn	玉米	*yùmǐ*
eggplant	茄子	*qiézi*
chili	辣椒	*làjiāo*
potato	土豆	*tǔdòu*
French fries	炸薯条	*zháshǔtiáo*
taro (root vegetable)	芋头	*yùtóu*
gingko nuts	银杏干果	*yínxìnggānguǒ*
tomato	番茄	*fānqié*
stir-fried tomato with egg	番茄炒鸡蛋	*fānqié chǎo jīdàn*
water chestnuts	荸荠	*bíqí*
cilantro	香菜	*xiāngcài*
garlic	大蒜	*dàsuàn*
ginger	生姜	*shēngjiāng*
cinnamon	肉桂	*ròuguì*
star anise	八角	*bājiǎo*
five-spice powder	五香粉	*wǔxiāngfěn*

SPECIALTIES

bean curd	豆腐	*dòufu*
dried bean curd	豆腐干	*dòufugān*
bean curd fried in batter	炸豆腐	*zhádòufu*
bean curd with prawns	豆腐虾仁	*dòufuxiārén*
"three-fresh" bean curd	三鲜豆腐	*sānxiāndòufu*
fermented black beans	豆豉	*dòuchǐ*
red bean paste	红豆沙	*hóngdòushā*
Sichuan chili paste	四川辣酱	*sìchuānlàjiàng*
soy bean paste	大豆酱	*dàdòujiàng*
Chinese ravioli	饺子	*jiǎozi*
steamed Chinese ravioli	蒸饺	*zhēngjiǎo*
fried Chinese ravioli	煎饺	*jiānjiǎo*
preserved eggs	皮蛋	*pídàn*
tofu	豆腐	*dòufu*
breaded tofu	煎豆腐	*jiāndòufu*
spicy tofu	辣豆腐	*làdòufu*
bird's nest	燕窝	*yànwō*

FRUIT

pineapple	菠萝	*bōluó*
guangdong sweet orange	广柑	*guǎnggān*
honeydew melon	哈密瓜	*hāmìguā*
tangerine	橘子	*júzi*
pear	梨	*lí*
lychee	荔枝	*lìzhī*
grape	葡萄	*pútáo*
guava	番石榴	*fānshíliu*
apple	苹果	*píngguǒ*
apricot	杏	*xìng*
banana	香蕉	*xiāngjiāo*
watermelon	西瓜	*xīguā*
lemon	柠檬	*níngméng*
lime	青柠	*qīngníng*
kiwi	猕猴桃	*míhóutáo*
cherry	樱桃	*yīngtáo*
Chinese dates	红枣	*hóngzǎo*
orange	橙子	*chéngzi*
mandarin orange	橘子	*júzi*
pomegranate	石榴	*shíliu*
Longan fruit	龙眼	*lóngyǎn*
peach	桃	*táo*
plum	梅子	*méizi*

DESSERTS

apple in hot toffee	拔丝苹果	*básīpíngguǒ*
ice cream	冰激淋	*bīngjīlín*
fruit salad	水果沙拉	*shuǐguǒshālā*
mixed fruit	水果拼盘	*shuǐguǒpīnpán*
"eight-treasure" rice dessert	八宝饭	*bābǎofàn*
rice pudding	米布丁	*mǐbùdīng*
almond bean curd	杏仁豆腐	*xìngréndòufu*
sweetened red bean paste	红豆沙	*hóngdòushā*
red bean paste pancakes	红豆沙饼	*hóngdòushābǐng*
cake	蛋糕	*dàngāo*
peanut cake	花生蛋糕	*huāshēngdàngāo*

DRINKS

water	水	*shuǐ*
sparkling water	汽水	*qìshuǐ*
fruit juice	果汁	*guǒzhī*
apple juice	苹果汁	*píngguǒzhī*
grapefruit juice	葡萄柚汁	*pútáoyòuzhī*
orange juice	橙汁	*chéngzhī*
tea	茶	*chá*
coffee	咖啡	*kāfēi*
cola	可乐	*kělè*
soda	苏打水	*sūdáshuǐ*
milk	牛奶	*niúnǎi*
soy milk	豆浆	*dòujiāng*
yogurt drink	乳酸饮品	*rǔsuānyǐnpǐn*
baiju (clear liquor)	白酒	*báijiǔ*
beer	啤酒	*píjiǔ*
wine	葡萄酒	*pútáojiǔ*
rice wine	米酒	*mǐjiǔ*
Chinese liqueurs	利口酒	*lìkǒujiǔ*

DICTIONARY ENGLISH–CHINESE

Chinese nouns can normally be used for either the singular or the plural. Verbs and adjectives are often used in combination with additional characters which modify the meaning (*see page 4*). Chinese word order can be different from English and you will need to look at the phrases in the book to develop a feel for how to use the vocabulary in context.

A

a (one) *yī*
à la carte *àn càidān diǎncài*
a little *yìdiǎn'er*
a lot *hěnduō*
abdomen *fù*
above *zài…shàngmian*
abseiling *xuánshéng xiàjiàng*
accelerator *jiāsùqì, yóumén*
accessories *měifà yòngpǐn*
accident *shìgù*
accommodation *zhùsù*
accountant *kuàijìshī*
accounts department *kuàijìbù*
accused *bèigào*
ache *téng*
achilles tendon *gēnjiàn*
acquaintance *shúrén*
across *yuèguò*
acrylic paint *bǐngxī yánliào*
actions *dòngzuò*
actor *yǎnyuán*
actress *nǚyǎnyuán*
acupuncture *zhēnjiǔ*
adaptor (plug) *chātóu zhuǎnhuànqì*
add (v) *jiā*
address *dìzhǐ*
adhesive bandage *chuàngkǒutiē*

adhesive tape *xiàngpígāo*
admission:
  admission charge *rùchǎngfèi*
  admission ticket *ménpiào*
advantage *fāqiúfāng zhànxiān*
advertisement *guǎnggào*
Afghanistan *āfùhàn*
Africa *fēizhōu*
after *yǐhòu*
afternoon *xiàwǔ*
aftershave *xūhòushuǐ*
aftersun *shàihòu hùfūyè*
again *zài*
agenda *yìchéng*
airbag *ānquánqìnáng*
air-conditioning *kōngtiáo*
air mail *hángkōngyóujiàn*
air mattress *chōngqì chuángdiàn*
airplane *fēijī*
airport *(fēi)jīchǎng*
aisle *guòdào*
alarm clock *nàozhōng*
Alaska *ālāsījiā*
Albania *ā'ěrbāníyà*
Algeria *ā'ěrjílìyà*
all *suǒyǒu*
  all the streets *suǒyǒu de jiēdào*
  that's all, thanks *hǎole, xièxie*

allergic *guòmǐn*

allergy *guòmǐn*

alley *xiǎoxiàng*

alligator *duǎnwěn'è*

all-purpose flour *zhōngjīnmiànfěn*

almond *xìngrén*

almost *chàbuduō*

alone *dāndú*

along *yánzhe*

alpine *gāoshān zhíwù*

already *yǐjīng*

also *yě*

altitude *gāodù*

always *zǒngshì*

am: I am *shì: wǒshì*

ambulance *jiùhùchē*

America *měiguó*

American (person) *měiguórén*

American football *měishì gǎnlǎnqiú*

amount *jīn'é*

amphibians *liǎngqī dòngwù*

amusement park *zhǔtígōngyuán*

anchor *máo*

and *hé*

angry *fènnù*

animal *dòngwù*

ankle *jiǎohuái*

anniversary *zhōunián*

annual *yìniánshēng (zhíwù)*

another (different) *lìngyīgè* (further) *yòuyīgè*

answer (v) *huídá*

answering machine *dálùjī*

ant *mǎyǐ*

antibiotics *kàngshēngsù*

antifreeze *fángdòngyè*

Antigua and Barbuda *āntíguā hé bābùdá*

anti-inflammatory *xiāoyányào*

antique store *gǔdǒngdiàn*

antiseptic *xiāodújì*

antiseptic wipe *xiāodú shījīn*

anything: anything else? *shénme:...qítā shénme ma?*

apartment *gōngyù*

apartment block *gōngyùlóu*

apéritif *kāiwèijiǔ*

appeal *shàngsù*

appearance *wàibiāo*

appendix *lánwěi*

appetizers *tóupán, kāiwèicài*

applaud (v) *gǔzhǎnghècǎi*

apple *píngguǒ*

apple juice *píngguǒzhī*

appliances *chúfáng diànqì*

application *yìngyòng chéngxù*

appointment *yùyuē*

appointment book *jìshìbù*

apricot *xìng*

April *sìyuè*

apron *wéiqún*

Arabian Sea *ālābó hǎi*

arc *hú*

arch *zúgǒng*

archery *shèjiàn*

architect *jiànzhùshī*

architecture (study) *jiànzhùxué*

are: you are *shì: nǐshì* we are *wǒmen shì* they are *tāmen shì*

area *miànjī*

arena *jìngjìchǎng*

Argentina *āgēntíng*

arm *shǒubì, gēbo*

armchair *fúshǒuyǐ*

Armenia *yàměiníyà*
armpit *yèwō*
armrest *fúshǒu*
aromatherapy *fāngxiāng liáofǎ*
around *zài…zhōuwéi*
arrangements *chāhuā*
arrest *dàibǔ*
arrival *dàodá*
arrive *dàodá*
arrow *jiàn*
art *yìshù*
artery *dòngmài*
art gallery *yìshùguǎn*
arthritis *guānjiéyán*
artichoke *cháoxiānjì*
artificial sweetener *rénzào tiánwèijì*
artist *huàjiā*
art store *yìshùpǐndiàn*
arugula *huǒjiàn*
ashtray *yānhuīgāng*
Asia *yàzhōu*
ask *wèn*
asleep: he's asleep *shuìzháole: tā shuìzháo le*
asparagus *lúsǔn*
assault *gōngjī*
assistant *zhùlǐ*
asthma *xiàochuǎn*
astronomy *tiānwénxué*
at *zài*
at the café *zài kāfēiguǎn*
athlete *tiánjìngxuǎnshǒu*
Atlantic Ocean *dàxī yáng*
ATM *tíkuǎnjī*
atmosphere *dàqìcéng*
attachment *fùjiàn*
attack *jìngōng*
attend (v) *cānjiā*

attic *gélóu*
attractions *míngshèng*
attractive *mírénde*
auburn *hónghèsè*
audience *guānzhòng*
August *bāyuè*
aunt (maternal) *yímā* (paternal) *gūmā*
Australasia *dàyángzhōu*
Australia *àodàlìyà*
Australian (person) *àodàlìyàrén*
Austria *àodìlì*
automatic *zìdòng*
automatic door *zìdòngmén*
automatic payment *zhíjiē jièjì*
avalanche *xuěbēng*
avenue *línyīndào*
avocado *èlí*
awful *zāotòule*
ax *xiāofángfǔ*
Azerbaijan *ā'sàibàijiāng*

B

baby *yīng'ér*
baby carriage *wòshìyīng'érchē*
baby changing room *yīng'érjiān*
baby monitor *yīng'ér jiānshìqì*
baby products *yīng'ér yòngpǐn*
baby sling *yīng'ér diàodài*
baby wipes *yīng'érshījīn*
back (body) *bèi*
backdrop *bèijìngmùbù*
backgammon *xīyáng shuānglùqí*
back seat *hòuzuò*
backpack *xiǎobāo*
back street *hòujiē*
bacon *xūnròu*
bad *huài, bùhǎo*
badge *jīnghuī*

badminton *yǔmáoqiú*

bag (for purchases, etc.) *dàizi*

bagel *yìngquānmiànbāo*

baggage *xíngli*

Bahamas *bāhāmǎ*

Bahrain *bālín*

bait *ěr*

bake (v) *hōngzhì*

baker *miànbāodiàn*

bakery *miànbāodiàn*

balcony *yángtái*

bald *tūdǐng*

ball *qiú*

ballet *bālěiwǔ*

balsamic vinegar *xiāngzhīcù*

Baltic Sea *bōluódì hǎi*

bamboo *zhúzi*

bamboo shoots *zhúsǔn*

banana *xiāngjiāo*

band (music) *yuèduì*

bandage *bēngdài*

Bangladesh *mèngjiālāguó*

banister *lóutī lángān*

bank *yínháng*

bank charge *yínháng shǒuxùfèi*

bank transfer *yínháng zhuǎnzhàng*

bar *jiǔbā*

Barbados *bābāduōsī*

barbecue *shāokǎojià*

barber *lǐfàdiàn*

bar code *tiáoxíngmǎ*

bark *shùpí*

barley *dàmài*

barn *gǔcāng*

bar snacks *jiǔbā xiǎochī*

bar stool *jiǔbāyǐ*

bartender *jiǔbǎo*

base *dǐ*

baseball *bàngqiú*

basement *dìxiàshì*

basil *luólè*

basket *lánzi*

basketball *lánqiú*

bass guitar *dīyīn jítā*

bassoon *bāsōngguǎn*

bat (v) *jīqiú*

bath mat *yùshì fánghuádiàn*

bathrobe *yùpáo*

bathroom *wèishēngjiān, yùshì*

bath towel *yùjīn*

bathtub *yùgāng*

battery *diànchí*

beach *hǎitān*

beach umbrella *zhēyángsǎn*

beaker *shāobēi*

beam *liáng*

beans *dòu*

bear *xióng*

beard *húxū*

beat *jiépāi*

beautiful *piàoliang*

beauty *měiróng yòngpǐn*

beauty products *měiróngchǎnpǐn*

beauty treatments *měirónghùlǐ*

because *yīnwéi*

bed *chuáng*

bed and breakfast *tígōng zhùsù hé zǎocān*

bedding *bèirù*

bed linen *chuángshàng yòngpǐn*

bedroom *wòshì*

bed runner *chuángqí*

bedside lamp *chuángtóudēng*

bedside table *chuángtóuguì*

bedspread *chuángdān*

bee *mìfēng*

beef *niúròu*

beer *píjiǔ*
beetle *jiǎkéchóng*
beet *tiáncài*
before *(zài)…yǐqián*
begin *kāishǐ*
beginner *chūxuézhě*
beginning *kāishǐ*
behind *(zài)…hòumiàn*
Belarus *bái'éluósī*
Belgium *bǐlìshí*
Belize *bólìzī*
bell *líng*
  (for door, school)
below *(zài)…xiàmiàn*
belt (clothing) *pídài*
bench *chángyǐ*
berry *jiāngguǒ*
best: the best *zuìhǎo*
better *gènghǎo*
between *(zài)…zhījiān*
beyond *chāochū*
Bhutan *bùdān*
bib *wéizuǐ*
bicep curl *èrtóujī xùnliàn*
biceps *èrtóujī*
bicycle *zìxíngchē*
bidet *jìngshēnpén*
big *dà*
big toe *dàzhǐ*
bike rack *zìxíngchē zhījià*
bikini *bǐjīní*
bill (banknote) *zhǐbì*
binoculars *shuāngtǒng wàngyuǎnjìng*
biology *shēngwùxué*
bird *niǎo*
birdwatching *guānniǎo*
birth *chūshēng*
birth certificate *chūshēng zhèngmíng*
birthday *shēngrì*
  happy birthday! *shēngrìkuàilè!*
bit *mǎ jiáo zi*
bite (injury) *yǎoshāng*
bite (v) *yǎo*
bitter (taste) *kǔ*
black *hēi*
  black tea *hóngchá*
  black coffee *hēikāfēi*
blackberry *hēiméi*
black currant *hēicùlì*
bladder *pángguāng*
blade *dāopiàn*
blanket *tǎnzi*
blazer *xiūxián shàngyī*
bleach *qīng jié jì*
blind *yǎnmáng*
blinds *bǎiyèchuāng*
blister *shuǐpào*
block *dǎng*
blocked (road, drain) *dǔzhùle*
blond *jīnfàde*
blood test *yànxiě*
blouse *nǚzhuāngchènshān*
blow dry (v) *chuīgān*
blowdryer *chuīfēngjī*
blue *lán*
bluebells *yěfēngxìnzǐ*
blueberry *lánméi*
blue cheese *lánwénnǎilào*
blues *lándiào yīnyuè*
blush *sāihóng*
board *fānbǎn*
board games *qípán yóuxì*
boarding gate *dēngjīmén*
boarding pass *dēngjīpái*
boat *chuán*
body *shēntǐ*

body lotion *rùnfūlù*
boil (v) *zhūfèi*
boiled *zhūde*
boiled egg *zhūjīdàn*
boiled rice *mǐfàn*
Bolivia *bōlìwéiyà*
bollard *ànbiānlánzhuāng*
bolt *ménshuān*
bone *gǔtou*
book (n) *shū*
book (v) *dìng*
book a flight (v) *dìngjīpiào*
bookshelf *shūjià*
bookstore *shūdiàn*
boot *xuēzi*
booties *duǎnxuē*
border (of country) *biānjiè*
bored *wúliáo*
boring *méijìn*
borrow (v) *jièrù*
boss *lǎobǎn*
both *liǎnggè dōu*
Botswana *bócíwǎnà*
bottle *píngzi*
bottle opener *kāipíngqì*
bottled water *píngzhuāng shuǐ*
bounce (v) *yùnqiú*
bouquet *huāshù*
boutique *fúzhuāngdiàn*
bow (nautical) *chuánshǒu*
bowl *wǎn*
bowling *bǎolíngqiú yùndòng*
bowling ball *bǎolíngqiú*
bow tie *lǐngjié*
box (n) *hézi*
boxer *quánjīshǒu*
box office *shòupiàochù*
boxing *quánjī*
boy *nánhái*

boyfriend *nánpéngyou*
bra *xiōngzhào*
bracelet *shǒuliàn*
braces *jīchǐ jiǎozhèngqì*
braid *máhuābiàn*
brain *nǎo*
brake *shāchē*
brake pedal *shāchētàbǎn*
branch *shùzhī*
branch (of company) *fēngōngsī*
brandy *báilándì*
brass *tóngguǎn yuèqì*
brazil *bāxī*
brazil nut *bāxīguǒ*
bread *miànbāo*
breadcrumbs *miànbāoxiè*
bread knife *miànbāodāo*
bread roll *xiǎoyuán miànbāo*
breakfast *zǎocān*
breakfast buffet *zìzhùzǎocān*
breakfast cereals
   zǎocān màipiàn
breast *xiōng*
breastfeed (v) *wèi mǔrǔ*
breathing *hūxī*
brick *zhuān*
bridge (over river, etc.) *qiáo*
Brie *bùlǐ gānlào*
briefcase *gōngwénbāo*
briefs *sānjiǎonèikù*
bring *dài*
brioche *nǎiyóugāodiǎn*
Britain *yīngguó*
British (adj) *yīngguó*
broadcast *guǎngbō*
broccoli *xīlánhuā*
broil (v) *shāokǎo*
broiled *shāo*
broken (out of order) *huàile*

(leg) *duànle*
bronze *tóngpái*
brooch *xiōngzhēn*
broom *chángbǐng
sàozhou*
broth *ròutāng*
brother (older) *gēge*
(younger) *dìdi*
brother-in-law
qīmèi(jiě)fū
brown *zōngsè*
brown rice *cāomǐ*
browse (v) *liúlǎn*
bruise *yūshāng*
brunette *shēnhèsè*
brush (v) *shuātóufa*
brush *shuāzi*
bubblebath *pàoyù*
bucket *shuǐtǒng*
buckle *yāodàikòu*
bud *huālěi*
Buddha *fó*
budget *yùsuàn*
buffet *zìzhùcān*
buggy *duǎntú xiǎochē*
build (v) *jiànzào*
building *jiànzhù*
built-in wardrobe
nèiqiànshì yīchú
bulb (plant) *qiújīng zhíwù*
bulb (light) *dēngpào*
Bulgaria *bǎojiālìyà*
bull *gōngniú*
bulldog clip *qiánglìzhǐjiā*
bulletin board *gōnggàolán*
bumper *bǎoxiǎngàng*
bun *xiǎoyuán dàngāo*
bunch *huāshù*
bungalow *píngfáng*

bungee jumping *bèngjí*
buoy *fúbiāo*
burger *hànbǎobāo*
burglar *qièzéi*
burglar alarm *fángdào jǐngbào*
burglary *rùshì dàoqiè*
Burma *miǎndiàn*
burn (n) *shāoshāng*
bus *gōngjiāochē*
bus driver *gōnggòngqìchē sījī*
bus station *gōngjiāochē
zǒngzhàn*
bus stop *gōngjiāochēzhàn*
bus ticket *gōnggòngqìchēpiào*
business *shēngyì*
on business *chūchāi*
business card *míngpiàn*
business lunch *gōngzuòwǔcān*
business partner
shēngyihuǒbàn
businessperson *shāngrén*
business suit *xīzhuāng*
business trip *shāngwùlǚxíng*
busy (street) *fánmáng*
(person) *(hěn)máng*
(phone line) *zhànxiàn*
but *dànshì*
butcher *ròudiàn*
butter *huángyóu*
buttercup *máogèn*
butterfly *diéyǒng*
butternut squash
dōngnánguā
button *niǔkòu*
buttonhole *kòuyǎn'ér*
buy *mǎi*
by *zuò*
by train/car *zuòhuǒchē /
zuòqìchē*

C

cab *jiàshǐshì*
cabbage *juǎnxīncài*
cabin (plane) *jīcāng*
cabinet (kitchen) *guìchú*
cable *diànlǎn*
cable TV *yǒuxiàn diànshì*
cactus *xiānrénzhǎng*
café *kāfēiguǎn, cānguǎn*
cake *dàngāo*
cake pan *dàngāo kǎomú*
cakes and desserts *gāodiǎn*
cake shop *dàngāodiàn*
calcium *gài*
calculator *jìsuànqì*
calendar *rìlì*
calf *niúdú*
call button *hūjiào ànniǔ*
call: what is this called? *jiào: zhèjiào shénme?*
calligraphy *shūfǎ*
Cambodia *jiǎnpǔzhài*
camcorder *biànxiéshì shèxiàngjī*
camel *luòtuo*
Camembert *kǎménbèi gānlào*
camera *zhàoxiàngjī*
camera case *xiàngjīhé*
cameraman *shèxiàngshī*
cameraphone *pāizhào shǒujī*
Cameroon *kāmàilóng*
camisole *jǐnshēn nèiyī*
camp (v) *lùyíng*
camp bed *xíngjūn chuáng*
Campari *kānpéilìjiǔ*
camper van *yěyíngchē*
campfire *yínghuǒ*
camping *lùyíng*
campus *xiàoyuán*
can (tin) *guàntou*

can opener *kāiguànqì*
can: can I...? *kěyǐ: wǒkěyǐ...ma?*
can you...? *nǐ kěyǐ...ma?*
he can't... *tā bù kěyǐ...*
Canada *jiānádà*
Canadian (person) *jiānádàrén*
canary *jīnsīquè*
candle *làzhú*
candy *tángguǒ*
candy store *tiánshídiàn*
canoe *dúmùzhōu*
canopy *zhēpéng*
Cantonese (adj) *guǎngdōng*
(language) *guǎngdōnghuà*
canvas *huàbù*
cap *màozi*
capacity *róngliàng*
capers *mǎbīngláng*
capital *shǒudū*
cappuccino *kǎbùqínuò kāfēi*
capsize (v) (chuán) *qīngfù*
captain *chuánzhǎng*
car *qìchē, chē*
car accident *chēhuò*
caramel *jiāotáng*
car rental *zūchēchù*
cart *tuīchē, xínglǐchē*
car wash *zìdòng xǐchēzhàn*
card (business) *míngpiàn*
cardamom *xiǎodòukòu*
cardboard *zhǐbǎn*
cardigan *yángmáoshān*
cards (playing) *zhǐpái*
careful: be careful! *xiǎoxīn!*
cargo *huòwù*
Caribbean Sea *jiālèbǐ hǎi*
carnival *kuánghuānjié / jiāʼniánhuáhuì*
carousel *xínglǐ chuánsòngdài*

carpenter *mùjiàng*
carpet *dìtǎn*
carrier *shǒutíshì yīng'érchuáng*
carrot *húluóbo*
carry out (food) *wàimài*
cartilage *ruǎngǔ*
carton *yìngzhǐhé*
cartoon *dònghuàpiān*
carve (v) *diāokè*
case *yǎnjìnghé*
cash (money) *xiànjīn*
cashew *yāoguǒ*
cash point *qǔkuǎnjī*
cash register *shōuyíntái*
cassette *cídài*
cast *juésè fēnpèi*
casual *biànzhuāng*
casual wear *biànzhuāng*
cat *māo*
catch (v) *jiēqiú*
caterpillar *máochóng*
cauliflower *huāyēcài, càihuā*
caution *jǐnshèn jiàshǐ*
cave *yándòng*
CD-drive *guāngqū*
CD player *CD bōfàngjī*
ceiling *tiānhuābǎn*
celebration *qìngzhùhuì*
celeriac *kuàigēnqín*
celery *qíncài*
cell *dānrénláofáng*
cell phone *shǒujī*
cello *dàtíqín*
centimeter *límǐ*
center (of town) *zhōngxīn*
cereal *gǔlèishípǐn*
chair *yǐzi*
   swivel chair *zhuànyǐ*
chairlift *lǎnchē diàoyǐ*

chalk *bái'è*
chamomile tea *júhuāchá*
champagne *xiāngbīnjiǔ*
championship *jǐnbiāosài*
change (verb: money) *huànqián, duìhuàn*
   (noun: money) *língqián*
   (verb: clothes, trains) *huàn*
change purse *qiánbāo*
changing bag *yīng'ér yīwùdài*
changing mat *huànyīdiàn*
channel *píndào*
charcoal *mùtàn*
charge *kònggào*
charger *chōngdiànqì*
chart *shǒushù jìlùbiǎo*
check (bill) *zhàngdān*
check *zhīpiào*
checkbook *zhīpiàoběn*
check card *zhīpiàokǎ*
checker *chūnàyuán*
check-in (hotel/airport) *bànlǐ rùzhù/dēngjī shǒuxù*
check-in desk *rùzhù/dēngjī shǒuxù bànlǐchù*
check-out *jiézhàng*
checkup *jiǎnchá*
Cheddar *qiědá gānlào*
cheek *liǎnjiá*
cheese *nǎilào*
chef *zhǔchú*
chemist *yàodiàn*
chemistry *huàxué*
cherry *yīngtáo*
cherry tomato *yīngtáofānqié*
chess *guójìxiàngqí*
chessboard *qípán*
chest (body) *xiōng*
chestnut *lìzi*

chest of drawers *wǔdǒuchú*
chest press *kuòxiōng*
chewing gum *kǒuxiāngtáng*
chick *xiǎojī*
chicken *jī*
  (meat) *jīròu*
chicken coop *jīshè*
chickenpox *shuǐdòu*
chickpeas *yīngzuǐdòu*
chicory *jújù*
child, children *háizi*
child lock *értóng ānquánsuǒ*
children *háizi*
children's clothing *tóngzhuāng*
children's department *értóng yòngpǐnbù*
children's ward *érkēbìngfáng*
child seat *értóngzuòyǐ*
child's meal *értóng tàocān*
Chile *zhìlì*
chili pepper *làjiāo*
chili powder *làjiāofěn*
chill *hánzhàn*
chimney *yāncōng*
chin *xiàbā*
China *zhōngguó*
China tea *zhōngguóchá*
Chinese (adj) *zhōngguó*
  (person) *zhōngguórén*
  (language) *zhōngwén*
  the Chinese *zhōngguórén*
Chinese New Year *chūnjié*
Chinese-style *zhōngshì*
chives *xìxiāngcōng*
chocolate *qiǎokèlì*
chocolate bar *qiǎokèlìbàng*
chocolate cake *qiǎokèlì dàngāo*
choir *shèngtán*
choke (v) *zhìxī*

chop *páigǔ*
chopstick(s) *kuàizi*
chorizo *suànwèilàcháng*
church *jiàotáng*
chutney *suānlàjiàng*
cigar *xuějiā*
cigarette *xiāngyān*
  pack of cigarettes *héyān*
cinnamon *ròuguì*
circle *yuánxíng*
citrus fruit *gānjúlèishuǐguǒ*
city *chéngshì*
clam *gélí*
clamp *jiáqián*
clarinet *dānhuángguǎn*
clasp *liànkòu*
classical music *gǔdiǎn yīnyuè*
classroom *jiàoshì*
claw *zhǎo*
clay *niántǔ*
clean (adj) *gānjìng*
cleaner (person) *qīngjiégōng*
cleanser *jiémiànshuǐ*
clear honey *yètǐfēngmì*
clever *cōngmíng*
client *kèhù*
cliff *xuányá*
climbing *pānyán,dēngshān*
climbing frame *pāndēngjià*
clinic *zhěnsuǒ*
clipboard *dài zhǐjiáde bǐjìbǎn*
clock *zhōng*
clock radio *shízhōng shōuyīnjī*
close (v) *guān*
close: to be close (near) *jìn*
closed *guānmén*
closet *yīchú*
clothes *yīfu*
clothes line *liàngyīshéng*

clothes peg *yījiā*
clothing *fúzhuāng*
cloud *yún*
cloudy *duōyún*
clove *suànbàn'er*
club *méihuā*
clutch *líhéqì*
coach (train) *chēxiāng*
  sleeper coach *yìngwòchēxiāng*
  ordinary coach *pǔtōngchēxiāng*
coal *méi*
coast *hǎi'àn*
coaster *bēidiàn*
coast guard *hǎi'àn jǐngwèiduì*
coat (overcoat) *dàyī*
  (jacket) *wàiyī*
coat hanger *guàyījià*
cockatoo *měiguàn yīngwǔ*
cockpit *jiàshǐcāng*
cockroach *zhāngláng*
cocktail *jīwěijiǔ*
cocktail shaker *jīwěijiǔ tiáozhìqì*
cocoa powder *kěkěfěn*
coconut milk *yēzizhī*
coconut *yēzi*
cod *xuěyú*
coffee *kāfēi*
coffee cup *kāfēibēi*
coffee with milk *niúnǎi kāfēi*
cog *liànpán*
coins *yìngbì*
cola *kělè*
cold (illness) *gǎnmào*
  (temperature) *lěng*
collar *yīlǐng*
collect/reverse charge call
  duìfāng fùkuǎn diànhuà
Colombia *gēlúnbǐyà*
color *yánsè*

colored pencils *cǎisèqiānbǐ*
comb *shūzi*
come *lái*
  please come! *láiba!*
comedy *xǐjùpiān*
comforter *yǔróngbèi*
comic (adj) *xǐjùde*
comic book *liánhuánmànhuà*
Communist Party *gòngchǎndǎng*
Communist Party member
  gòngchǎndǎngyuán
compact *fěnhé*
company (firm) *gōngsī*
complexion *fūsè*
complicated *fùzá*
computer *diànnǎo, jìsuànjī*
computer repair shop
  diànnǎo xiūlǐdiàn
concealer *zhēxiágāo*
concert *yīnyuèhuì*
concussion *nǎozhèndàng*
conditioner *hùfàsù*
condom *bìyùntào*
conductor *zhǐhuī*
cone *zhuīxínggélídūn*
conference *yántǎohuì*
constipation *biànmì*
construction site *jiànzhùgōngdì*
construction worker
  jiànzhùgōngrén
consulate *lǐngshìguǎn*
contact lenses *yǐnxíngyǎnjìng*
contract (n) *hétong*
controls *cāozuòzhuāngzhì*
convenience food
  fāngbiàn shípǐn
convertible *chǎngpéngchē*
cook (chef) *chúshī*
cookie *bǐnggān*

cool (day, weather) *liángshuǎng*
copper *tóng*
corkscrew *básāizuàn*
corn *tiányùmǐ*
corner (street) *jiǎoluò*
corridor *zǒuláng*
cost *jiàqián*
  what does it cost? *zhèyào duōshǎoqián?*
cotton *miánhuā*
cotton wool *yàomián*
cough *késòu*
countertop *cāozuòtái*
country (nation) *guójiā*
courier *sùdì*
cow *niú*
crab *pángxiè*
cramps *jìngluán*
cranberry *mànyuèjú*
crayfish *xiǎolóngxiā*
cream (to eat) *nǎiyóu*
credit card *xìnyòngkǎ*
crew *chúanyuán*
crib *yīng'érchuáng*
cricket *xīshuài*
cricket ball *bǎnqiú*
crime *fànzuì*
criminal record *fànzuìjìlù*
Croatia *kèluódìyà*
crochet *gōuzhī*
crocodile *èyú*
crop (agr.) *zhuāngjia*
crossing (street) *bānmǎxiàn*
crow *wūyā*
crowd *rénqún*
crowded *yōngjǐ*
Cuba *gǔbā*
cuff *chōngqì xiùdài*
cufflinks *xiùkòu*

Cultural Revolution
  wénhuà dàgémìng
cumin *kūmíng, xiǎohuíxiāng*
cup *bēizi*
  a cup of coffee *yībēikāfēi*
cured *fēnggànde*
curling tongs *juǎnfàqián*
currency exchange *wàibì duìhuànchù*
curry *gālí*
curtains *chuānglián*
curved *wānqū*
custard *dànnǎigāo*
customer service department
  kèhùfúwùbù
customs *hǎiguān*
cut (wound) *gēshāng*
  (v) *qiē*
cuticle *(zhǐjiaxia) biǎopí*
cutting board *ànbǎn*
cycling *qí zìxíngchē*
cyclist *qí zìxíngchē de rén*
cylinder *yuánzhùtǐ*
Cyprus *sàipǔlùsī*
Czech Republic *jiékègònghéguó*

D

dairy (foods) *rǔzhìpǐn*
dairy products *rǔzhìpǐn*
dam *shuǐbà*
dance *wǔqǔ*
dancer *wǔdǎoyǎnyuán*
dancing *tiàowǔ*
danger *wēixiǎn*
dangerous *wēixiǎn*
dark (skin) *fūsè jiàoshēn*
dark (dim light) *hēi'àn*
dartboard *bǎpán*
darts *fēibiāo*

date yēzǎo
daughter nǚér
dawn fúxiǎo
day tiān
day planner rìzhì
dead sǐle
deaf ěrlóng
debit card yínhángkǎ
December shí'èryuè
deck lù tái
decoration zhuāngshì
deep shēn
deep end shēnshuǐqū
deep-fried yóuzhá
defrost (v) jiědòng
delayed wǎndiǎn
delicatessen shúshídiàn
delicious hǎochī
delivery jiāofù
Denmark dānmài
dentist yáyī
deodorant chúchòujì
department xì
department (of company) bùmén
department store bǎihuòshāngdiàn
departure lounge hòujīdàtīng
departure(s) chūfā
desert shāmò
designer shèjìshī
desk bàngōngzhuō
dessert cānhòu tiándiǎn
destination mùdìdì
detergent qīngjiéjì
detour ràoxíngdàolù
develop (film) chōngxǐ
diabetes tángniàobìng
dial (v) bōhào

diapers zhǐniàokù
diaphragm gémó
diarrhea fùxiè
dice tóuzi
dictionary zìdiǎn
die sǐ
diesel cháiyóu
different bùtóng
difficult kùnnán
digital radio shù zì guǎng bō
dinghy xiàngpítǐng
dinner wǎncān
dining car cānchē
dining room cāntīng
dinner party wǎnyàn
dinner plate zhèngcān yòngpán
dipstick liàngyóujì
dirty zāng
disabled cánjí
disco dísīkē
discuss (v) tǎolùn
disembark (v) líchuán dēngàn
dishwasher xǐwǎnjī
disposable camera yīcìxìng xiàngjī
disposable razor yícìxìng tìxūdāo
distance jùlí
district xíngzhèngqū
dive (v) tiàoshuǐ
divorce líhūn
divorced líhūnle
DJ liúxíngyīnyuè jiémù zhǔchírén
do zuò
doctor yīshēng
document wénjiàn
documentary jìlùpiàn
dog gǒu
dollar měiyuán
dolphin hǎitún

Dominican Republic *duōmǐníjiā*
dominoes *duōmǐnuò gǔpái*
don't! *búyào!*
  do not enter *jìnzhǐ tōngxíng*
donkey *lǘ*
door *mén*
  (vehicle) *chēmén*
doorbell *ménlíng*
door lock *ménsuǒ*
doormat *méndiàn*
dosage *jìliàng*
double room *shuāngrénjiān*
dough *shēng miàntuán*
down *xiàngxià*
down: down there *xiàmiàn*
download (v) *xiàzǎi*
dragonfly *qīngtíng*
draining board *cānjù lìshuǐjià*
draw (v) *huà*
drawer *chōutì*
drawing *sùmiáo*
dress (woman's) *liányīqún*
dressing table *shūzhuāngtái*
drill *yázuàn*
drink (v) *hē*
drinking water *yǐnyòngshuǐ*
drinks *yǐnliào*
drip *jìng mài dī yè*
drive (v) *jiàshǐ*
driver *sījī*
driver's seat *jiàshǐxí*
driving license *jiàshǐzhízhào*
drops (medicinal) *dījì*
drown (v) *nìshuǐ*
drugstore (pharmacy)
  yàojìshī
drum kit *jiàzigǔ*
drunk *hēzuìle*
dry *gān*

dry cleaner *gānxǐdiàn*
duck *yā*
  (meat) *yāròu*
duffel bag *lǚxíngdài*
dumplings *jiǎozi*
dusk *huánghūn*
duty-free store *miǎnshuìdiàn*
DVD *DVD guāngpán*
dynasty *cháodài*
  the Ming/Ch'ing Dynasty
  míngcháo/ qīngcháo

E

each *měi(yī)gè*
eagle *yīng*
ear *ěrduo*
ear ache *ěrtòng*
early *zǎo*
earphones *ěrjī*
earring *ěrhuán*
earthquake *dìzhèn*
east *dōng*
easy *róngyì*
eat (v) *chī*
eat-in *diànnèi yòngcān*
eating out *wàichū jiùcān*
economy (class) *jīngjìcāng*
eczema *shīzhěn*
edge *bǎnbiān*
egg *jīdàn*
egg cup *dànbēi*
egg noodles *jīdànmiàn*
eggplant *qiézi*
Egypt *āijí*
eight *bā*
eighteen *shíbā*
either...or...
  búshì...jiùshì...
elastic *yǒutánxìngde*

elbow *zhǒu*
electric blanket *diànrètǎn*
electric guitar *diànjítā*
electrician *diàngōng*
electricity *diàn*
electric shock *diànjī*
electronics store
  diànzǐshāngdiàn
elephant *xiàng*
elevator *diàntī*
eleven *shíyī*
El Salvador *sà'ěrwǎduō*
else: something else
  qítā: qítā shénme
anything else?
  …qítā shénme ma?
  somewhere else *biéde dìfāng*
email *diànzǐyóujiàn*
email address
  diànzǐyóujiàn dìzhǐ
embarrassed *gāngà*
embarrassing *gāngà*
embassy *dàshǐguǎn*
emergency *jǐnjíqíngkuàng*
emergency exit *jǐnjí chūkǒu*
emergency ward *jízhěnshì*
emigrate (v) *yímín*
emperor *huángdì*
empty *kōng*
encore *zàiláiyīcì*
encyclopedia
  bǎikēquánshū
end (n) *mòduān*
end *jiéshù*
engaged (to be married)
  dìnghūnle
engaged/busy *zhànxiàn*
engine *fādòngjī*
engineer *gōngchéngshī*

engineering (study)
  gōngchéngxué
England *yīnggélán*
English (person) *yīngguórén*
(language) *yīngwén*
enough *gòule*
entrance *rùkǒu*
entrance/exit ramp *chàdào*
entrance ticket *ménpiào*
envelope *xìnfēng*
environment *huánjìng*
epilepsy *diānxián*
eraser *xiàngpí*
espresso *yìshìnóngsuō kāfēi*
estimate *gūsuàn*
Estonia *àishā'níyà*
estuary *hékǒu*
Europe *ōuzhōu*
evening *wǎnshàng*
evening menu *wǎncāncàidān*
every *měi(yī)gè*
  every day *měitiān*
  every week *měi(gè)xīngqī*
everyone *měigèrén*
everything *měijiànshì*
everywhere *měigèdìfāng*
exactly *zhǔnquède*
excellent *hǎojíle*
excess baggage
  chāozhòng xíngli
exchange (goods)
  gēnghuàn
exchange rate *huìlǜ*
excited *huān xǐ*
excursion *duǎntúlǚxíng*
excuse me (to get attention)
  láojià, qǐngwèn
  (pardon?) *qǐng zàishuō yībiàn?*
excuse me *bàoqiàn, dǎrǎoyíxià*

exhaust (car, etc.) *páiqìguǎn*
exhaust pipe *páiqìguǎn*
exhibition *zhǎnlǎn*
exit *chūkǒu*
expensive *guì*
expiration date *yǒuxiào qīxiàn*
eye *yǎnjīng*
eyebrow *méi*
eyelash *jiémáo*
eyeliner *yǎnxiànyè*
eye shadow *yǎnyǐng*
eye test *shìlì jiǎnchá*
eye-witness *mùjìzhě*

F

fabric *bùpǐ*
fabric conditioner *zhīwù róushùnjì*
face *liǎn*
factory *gōngchǎng*
faint (v) *yūndǎo*
fall (season) *qiūtiān*
family *jiātíng*
family room *jiātíngfáng*
fan (mechanical) *fēngshàn*
   (hand-held) *shànzi*
far (away) *yuǎn*
fare *chēpiào*
farm *nóngchǎng*
farmer *nóngmín*
fashion *shízhuāng*
fast *kuài*
fastening *kòuhuán*
fast food *kuàicān*
fat *féiròu*
fat (person) *pàng*
father *fùqīn*
   my father *wǒde fùqīn*

faucet *shuǐlóngtóu*
fava beans *cándòu*
fax *chuánzhēn*
fax machine *chuánzhēnjī*
February *èryuè*
feel *gǎnjué*
   I feel hot *wǒ gǎnjué rè*
female *nǚxìng*
fence *líba*
ferry *dùchuán*
ferry terminal *dùchuán mǎtóu*
festival *jiérì*
fever *fāshāo*
few: a few *yīxiē*
fiancé(e) *wèihūn fū/qī*
field *tiándì*
   (rice, paddy) *dàotián*
fifteen *shíwǔ*
figures (e.g. sales) *jīn'é*
Fiji *fěijì*
file *cuòdāo*
fillet *lǐjiròu*
film (camera) *jiāojuǎn*
find *zhǎo*
finger *shǒuzhǐ*
Finland *fēnlán*
fins *jiǎopǔ*
fire *huǒ*
   there's a fire! *zháohuǒle!*
fire alarm *huǒzāi bàojǐngqì*
fire department *xiāofángduì*
fire truck *xiāofángchē*
fire escape *xiāofángtōngdào*
fire extinguisher *mièhuǒqì*
firelighter *yǐnhuǒwù*
fireplace *bìlú*
first *dìyī*
first aid *jíjiù*
first-aid box *jíjiùxiāng*

first floor *yīlóu*
fish *yú*
fisherman *yúmín*
fishing *diàoyú*
fishing boat *yúchuán*
fishing rod *yúgān*
fish seller *shuǐchǎndiàn*
fitness *jiànshēn*
fitting rooms *gēngyīshì*
five *wǔ*
flag *qízi*
flash (for camera) *shǎnguāngdēng*
flashlight *shǒudiàntǒng*
flask *shāopíng*
flat (adj) *píngtǎn*
flat tyre *biětāi*
flavor *wèidào*
flea *tiàozǎo*
flight *hángbān*
flight attendant *kōngchèng rényuán*
flight number *hángbānhào*
flip-flops *píngdǐ rénzì tuōxié*
float *fúbǎn*
flood *hóngshuǐ*
floor (of room) *dìbǎn*
  (storey) *lóucéng*
florist *huādiàn*
flower *huā*
flowerbed *huātán*
flowers *huā*
flu *liúgǎn*
flute *xìchángxíngmiànbāo*
fly (insect) *cāngyíng*
fly (v) *fēi*
fog *wù*
folder *wénjiànjiā*

folk music *mínsúyīnyuè*
fond: I'm fond of
  xǐhuān: wǒ xǐhuān
food *shíwù*
food poisoning *shíwù zhòngdú*
foot *jiǎo*
  foot treatment (spa) *zúliáo*
footpath *xiǎodào*
for: for her *wèi: wèi tā*
  that's for me *zhèshì gěiwǒde*
  a bus for... *qù...de gōngjiāochē*
forbidden *jìnzhǐ*
Forbidden City *gùgōng*
forehead *qián'é*
foreign currency *wàibì*
foreigner *wàiguórén*
forest *sēnlín*
fork *chāzi*
forward *qiánfēng*
foundation *fěndǐ*
fountain *pēnquán*
four *sì*
fourteen *shísì*
fox *húli*
fracture *gǔzhé*
fragile *yìsǔnhuài*
fragranced *xiāng*
frame *zhìjià*
freckle *quèbān*
free *kòngxián*
free (of charge) *miǎnfèi*
  to be free (available) *yǒukòng*
freeze *jiébīng*
freezer *bīngguì*
French fries *zhátǔdòutiáo*
French press *kāfēihú*
French stick *gùnzimiànbāo*
Friday *xīngqīwǔ*
fried *chǎo*

fried noodles *chǎomiàn*
fried rice *chǎofàn*
friend *péngyou*
friendly *yǒuhǎo*
friendship store *yǒuyì shāngdiàn*
from: from Beijing to Shanghai
  cóng: cóng běijīng dào shànghǎi
front *qiánmiàn*
front door *qiánmén*
frost *shuāng*
frozen *lěngdòngde*
frozen foods *lěngdòng shípǐn*
fruit *shuǐguǒ*
fruit juice *guǒzhī*
fry (v) *kǎozhì*
fry (deep fry) *zhá*
  (stir fry) *chǎo*
frying pan *jiānguō*
fuel tank *rányóuxiāng*
full *mǎn*
  I'm full *wǒ bǎo le*
funny (strange) *qíguài*
  (amusing) *hǎoxiào*
furniture *jiājù*
fusebox *bǎoxiǎnsī*

G

garden *huāyuán*
gardener *yuándīng*
gardens (public) *yuánlín*
garlic *dàsuàn*
gas *méiqì*
gasoline *qìyóu*
gas pump *qìyóubèng*
gas station *jiāyóuzhàn*
gate *mén*
gate (airport, etc.) *dēngjīkǒu*
gearbox *biànsùxiāng*
gear shift *biànsùgǎn*

Germany *déguó*
get (obtain) *dédào*
get (fetch) *qǔ*
  (train, bus, etc) *zuò*
get: have you got...?
  yǒu: nǐ yǒu...ma?
get in (to car) *shàngchē*
  (arrive) *dàodá*
get up (in morning)
  qǐchuáng
gift *lǐwù*
gin *dùsōngzǐjiǔ*
ginger *jiāng*
giraffe *chángjǐnglù*
girl *nǚhái*
girlfriend *nǚpéngyou*
give *gěi*
glad *gāoxìng*
glass (for drinking) *bōlíbēi*
  (material) *bōlí*
glasses (spectacles) *yǎnjìng*
  wearing glasses *dàiyǎnjìng*
gloves *shǒutào*
glue *jiāoshuǐ*
go *qù*
gold *huángjīn*
golf/golfer *gāo'ěrfū*
golf clubs *gāo'ěrfū qiúgān*
golf course *gāo'ěrfū qiúchǎng*
good *hǎo*
good afternoon *xiàwǔhǎo*
goodbye *zàijiàn*
good evening *wǎnshànghǎo*
good morning *zǎoshànghǎo*
good night *wǎn'ān*
gorge *xiágǔ*
government *zhèngfǔ*
GPS receiver *wèixīng dǎohángyí*
gram *kè*

grandchildren
sūnzǐnǚ / wàisūnzǐnǚ
granddaughter
(son's daughter) *sūnnǚ*
(daughter's daughter)
wàisūnnǚ
grandfather
(paternal) *yéye*
(maternal) *wàigōng*
grandmother
(paternal) *nǎinai*
(maternal) *wàipó*
grandparents *zǔfùmǔ /*
wàizǔfùmǔ
grandson (son's son) *sūnzi*
(daughter's son) *wàisūnzi*
grapes *pútáo*
grass *cǎo*
gray *huīsè*
great: that's great! *jíhǎo: hǎojíle*
Great Britain *dàbùlièdiān*
Great Wall *chángchéng*
Greece *xīlà*
green *lǜ*
green Chinese onion *dàcōng*
green tea *lǜchá*
groceries *shípǐn záhuò*
ground *mósuìde*
guarantee *bǎoxiū*
guest *kèrén*
guide *zhǐnán, dǎoyóu*
guided tour *yǒu xiàngdǎo*
jiǎngjiě de yóulǎn
guitarist *jí tā shǒu*
gun (pistol) *shǒuqiāng*
(rifle) *qiāng*
gutter (of house) *páishuǐcáo*
gym *jiànshēnfáng*

H

hail *bīngbáo*
hair *tóufa*
haircut *lǐfà*
hairdresser *měifàshī*
hairdye *rǎnfàjì*
hairspray *dìngxíngshuǐ*
hair straighteners *zhí fà qì*
half *bàn*
half an hour *bànxiǎoshí*
half past one *yīdiǎnbàn*
ham *huǒtuǐ*
hamburger *hànbǎobāo*
hammer *chuízi*
hammock *diàochuáng*
hamstring *huòpángjiàn*
hand *shǒu*
handbag *shǒutídài*
handkerchief *shǒujuàn*
handle (n) *bǎshǒu*
handsome *yīngjùn*
hand towel *máojīn*
handyman *xiūlǐgōng*
happen *fāshēng*
happy *kuàilè*
harbor *gǎngkǒu*
hard (material) *yìng*
(difficult) *nán*
hard candy *yìngtáng*
hard drive *yìngpán*
hard hat *ānquánmào*
hardware store *wǔjīndiàn*
hat *lǐmào*
hate: I hate... *tǎoyàn: wǒ tǎoyàn*
have *yǒu*
do you have...? *nǐ yǒu ...ma?*
I have... *wǒ yǒu...*
I don't have... *wǒ méiyǒu...*
hayfever *kūcǎorè*

he *tā*
head *tóu*
headache *tóutòng*
head office *zǒnggōngsī*
headlight(s) *qiándēng*
headphones *ěrjī*
health insurance
　jiànkāngbǎoxiǎn
hear *tīngjiàn*
hearing aid
　zhùtīngqì
heart *xīnzàng*
heart attack *xīnjī gěngsè*
heart condition *xīnzàngbìng*
heat(ing) *gōngnuǎn*
heavy *zhòng*
heavy cream *gāozhīfángnǎiyóu*
heel (shoe) *xiégēn*
　(foot) *jiǎohòugēn*
helicopter *zhíshēng fēijī*
hello *nǐhǎo*
　(on the phone) *wéi*
helmet *tóukuī*
help *qiúzhù*
help (v) *bāngzhù*
help! *jiùmìng!*
hepatitis *gānyán*
her (possessive) *tāde*
　(object) *tā*
herb *yàocǎo*
herbs (cooking) *xiāngcǎo*
　(medicine) *cǎoyào*
here *zhèlǐ, zhèr*
　here you are *gěinǐ*
hers *tāde*
hi! *nǐhǎo!*
high *gāo*
high chair *gāojiǎoyǐzi*
highway *gāosùgōnglù*

hiking *yuǎnzú*
hill *qiūlíng*
him *tā*
hip *kuān*
his *tāde*
HIV positive *àizībìng yángxìng*
hobby *àihào*
hockey *qūgùnqiú*
hockey stick *qūgùnqiú bàng*
home *jiā*
homosexual *tóngxìngliàn*
honey *fēngmì*
Hong Kong *xiānggǎng*
hood *fēngmào*
hood (of car) *yīnqínggài*
horn (car, etc.) *lǎbā*
horrible *kěpà*
horror film *kǒngbùpiān*
horse *mǎ*
horseback riding *qí mǎ*
hospital *yīyuàn*
host *dōngdàozhǔ*
hot (temperature) *rè*
　(spicy) *là*
hot chocolate *rèqiǎokèlì*
hot drinks *rèyǐn*
hotel (superior, for foreigners)
　jiǔdiàn
　(small) *lǚguǎn*
hot spa *wēnquán*
hot-water bottle
　nuǎnshuǐdài
hour *xiǎoshí*
house *fángzi*
household products
　jiātíngyòngpǐn
hovercraft *qìdiànchuán*
how? *zěnme?*
　how are you? *nǐ zěnmeyàng?*

how much? *duōshǎo?*
　(money) *duōshǎoqián?*
humid *cháoshī*
hundred *bǎi*
Hungary *xiōngyálì*
hungry: I'm hungry *è: wǒ è le*
hurricane *jùfēng*
hurry: I'm in a hurry
　jí: wǒ hěnjí
hurt *tòng*
husband *zhàngfū*

I

I *wǒ*
ice *bīng*
ice cream *bīngjīlíng*
ice-skating *liūbīng*
if *rúguǒ*
immediately *mǎshàng*
immigration *yí mín*
impossible *bùkěnéng*
in *zài*
　in English *yòng yīngyǔ*
inbox *shōujiànxiāng*
inch *yīngcùn*
India *yìndù*
Indian Ocean *yìndù yáng*
indigestion *xiāohuà bùliáng*
Indonesia *yìndùníxīyà*
inexpensive *piányi*
infection *gǎnrǎn*
inflatable ring *yóuyǒngquān*
information *xìnxī*
information desk *wènxùnchù*
inhaler (for asthma, etc) *xīrùqì*
injection *zhùshè*
injury *chuāngshāng*
insect repellent *qūchóngjì*
inside *zài…lǐmiàn*

instructions *shǐyòng shuōmíng*
instruments *yuèqì*
insurance *bǎoxiǎn*
interesting *yǒuyìsi*
interchange *shízìlùkǒu*
intermission *mùjiānxiūxī*
internet *yīntèwǎng*
internet café *wǎngbā*
interpret *kǒuyì*
interpreter *kǒuyìyuán*
intersection *shí zì lù kǒu*
into *dào…lǐ*
inventory *huòwù qīngdān*
invitation *yāoqǐng*
invoice *fāpiào*
Iran *yīlǎng*
Iraq *yīlākè*
Ireland *àiěrlán*
iron (for clothes) *yùndǒu*
ironing board *yùnyībǎn*
is *shì*
　he/she/it is *tā /tā /tā shì*
island *dǎo*
it *tā*
　it's expensive *zhè hěnguì*
Italy *yìdàlì*

J

jack (for car)
　qiānjīndǐng
jacket *jiákè, wàitào*
jade *yù*
jam *guǒjiàng*
Jamaica *yámǎijiā*
January *yīyuè*
Japan *rìběn*
jar *guǎngkǒupíng*
jasmine tea *huāchá*
jaw *hé*

jazz *juéshìyuè*
jeans *niúzǎikù*
jellyfish *shuǐmǔ*
jet skiing *shuǐshàng mótuō*
jeweler *shǒushìdiàn*
jewelry *shǒushì*
jigsaw *lòuhuājù*
jigsaw puzzle *pīntú*
job *gōngzuò*
joint *guānjié*
jogging *mànpǎo*
journal *zázhì*
journalist *xīnwén jìzhě*
juice *zhīyè*
July *qīyuè*
jump *tiào*
June *liùyuè*
junk (boat) *shānbǎn*
just (only) *jǐnjǐn*
just one *jiù yīgè*

K

karaoke *kǎlā OK*
karaoke bar *kǎlā OK jiǔbā*
kayak *pífá*
Kenya *kěnníyà*
ketchup *fānqiéjiàng*
kettle *diànshuǐhú*
key *yàoshi*
keyboard *jiànpán*
kick (v) *tīqiú*
kidney *shènzàng*
kilo *gōngjīn*
kilogram *qiānkè*
kilometer *gōnglǐ*
king prawn *dàduìxiā*
kitchen *chúfáng*
knee *xī*
knife *dāo*

know: I don't know
   zhīdào: wǒ bù zhīdào
knuckle *zhǐguānjié*
Korea: North Korea
   cháoxiǎn: běicháoxiǎn
   South Korea *hánguó*

L

labels *qiāntiáo*
ladder *xiāofángtī*
ladle *chángbǐngsháo*
lady *nǔshì*
lake *hú*
lamb *gāoyángròu*
lamb (meat) *yángròu*
lamp *dēng*
landlord *fángdōng*
lane *xiǎoxiàng*
languages *yǔyán*
Laos *lǎowō*
laptop (computer) *bǐjìběn*
   diànnǎo
large *dà*
last (previous) *shàng(yī)gè*
   last month *shànggèyuè*
   (final) *zuìhòu*
last name *xìng*
last week *shàngzhōu*
last year *qùnián*
late (at night) *wǎn*
   (behind schedule) *chíle*
later *yǐhòu*
laugh (v) *xiào*
laundromat *tóubìshì*
   zìdòngxǐyīdiàn
law (study) *fǎlù*
lawyer *lùshī*
leaded *hánqiān*
leaflets *xuānchuányè*

learn (v) *xuéxí*

lecture (university) *jiǎngzuò*

lecture theater *jiētī jiàoshì*

lecturer (university) *dàxuéjiǎngshī*

left (not right) *zuǒ*

on the left *zàizuǒbiān*

leg *tuǐ*

leisure *xiūxián*

leisure time *xiūxián shíjiān*

lemon *níngméng*

lemon grass *níngméngcǎo*

lemonade *níngméng shuǐ*

length *cháng*

lens *jìngtóu*

lens cap *jìngtóugài*

letter (in post) *xìnjiàn*

lettuce *shēngcài*

level (n) *shuǐpíngyí*

lever *shǒubǐng*

library *túshūguǎn*

lid *gàizi*

lie down *tǎng*

life *shēnghuó*

life jacket *jiùshēngyī*

life ring *jiùshēngquān*

ligament *rèndài*

light (n) *dēng*

have you got a light? *néng jiègèhuǒ ma?*

(not heavy) *qīng*

light bulb *dēngpào*

lighter *dǎhuǒjī*

lightning *shǎndiàn*

light switch *chēdēng kāiguān*

like: I'd like... *xiǎng: wǒ xiǎng yào*

I like *wǒ xǐhuān*

the one like that *xiàng nàge yīyàngde*

lime *duànshù*

line (phone) *diànhuàxiàn*

outside line *wàixiàn*

(transport route) *lù de shāngdiàn*

lip *chún*

lipstick *kǒuhóng*

liquor *jiǔjīng*

liquor store *yǒu màijiǔ zhízhào*

liquid *yètǐ*

literature (study) *wénxué*

Lithuania *lìtáowǎn*

liter *shēng*

little finger *xiǎozhǐ*

little toe *xiǎozhǐ*

little *xiǎo*

just a little *jiù yīdiǎnr*

liver *gān*

livestock *jiāchù*

living roon *kètīng*

load (v) *zhuāngrù*

loaf *miànbāokuài*

loan *jièchū*

lobby *dàtīng*

lobster *lóngxiā*

lock *suǒ*

lockers *suǒguì*

long *cháng*

lose: I've lost my... *diū: wǒ diūle wǒde...*

lost property *shīwù zhāolǐngchù*

lot: a lot *xǔduō*

a lot of money *xǔduōqián*

loud *dàshēng*

love *ài*

love: I love you *ài: wǒ ài nǐ*

I'd love to come *wǒ hěnxiǎng lái*

lovely (person) *kěài*
  (thing) *měimiàode*
low *dī*
luck *yùnqì*
  good luck! *zhù nǐ hǎoyùn!*
luggage *xíngli*
luggage rack *xínglijià*
luggage storage *xíngli jìcúnchù*
lunch *wǔcān*
lunch menu *wǔ cān cài dān*
lychee *lìzhī*

M

mackerel *qīngyú*
magazine *zázhì*
magnet *cítiě*
maid service *kèfáng qīngjié fúwù*
mailbox *xìnxiāng*
mail carrier *yóudìyuán*
main courses *zhǔcài*
make *zuò*
makeup *huàzhuāng*
Malaysia *mǎláixīyà*
male *nánxìng, nánshì*
man *nánrén*
manager *jīnglǐ*
Mandarin *pǔtōnghuà*
mango *mángguǒ*
manicure *zhǐjia hùlǐ*
map *dìtú*
maple syrup *fēngtángjiāng*
March *sānyuè*
marinated *cùzìde*
market *shìchǎng*
marmalade *júzijiàng*
married *yǐhūn*
marshmallow *miánhuāruǎntáng*

martial arts *wǔshù*
mascara *jiémáogāo*
mask (diving) *qiánshuǐmiànzhào*
massage *ànmó*
matches *huǒchái*
material (cloth) *bù*
matter: what's the matter?
  (asking about illness) *nǎlǐ bù shūfu?*
May *wǔyuè*
maybe *yěxǔ*
mayonnaise *dànhuángjiàng*
me *wǒ*
  it's for me *zhè shì gěiwǒde*
measles *mázhěn*
measure *liángbēi*
measuring cup *liánghú*
measuring spoon *liángchí*
meat *ròu*
meatballs *ròuwán*
mechanic *jīxièshī*
medicine (medication) *yào*
medicine (study) *yīxué*
Mediterranean Sea *dìzhōng hǎi*
meet (someone) *jiàn*
meeting *huìyì*
melon *guā*
memory (computer) *nèicún*
memory card *jìyìkǎ*
men's clothing *nánzhuāng*
men's toilets *náncèsuǒ*
menswear *nánzhuāng*
menu *càidān*
  set menu *tàocān*
messages *liúyán*
metal *jīnshǔ*
meter (length) *mǐ*
Mexico *mòxīgē*
microphone *huàtǒng*

microwave *wēibōlú*

middle-aged *zhōngnián*

middle: in the middle
  zhōngjiān: zài zhōngjiān

midnight: at midnight *bànyè*

migraine *piāntóutòng*

mile *yīnglǐ*

milk *niúnǎi*

milligram *háokè*

milliliter *háoshēng*

million *bǎiwàn*

ground meat *ròuxiàn*

mine: it's mine
  wǒde: zhè shì wǒde

mineral water
  kuàngquánshuǐ

minibar *xiǎobīngxiāng*

minute *fēnzhōng*

mirror *jìngzi*

Miss *xiǎojiě*

mistake *cuòwù*

mixed salad *shíjǐnshālā*

modem *tiáozhìjiětiáoqì*

moisturizer *bǎoshīshuāng*

Monday *xīngqīyī*

money *qián*

Mongolia *ménggǔ*

  Inner Mongolia *nèiménggǔ*

  Outer Mongolia *wàiménggǔ*

monkey *hóuzi*

monkfish *ānkāngyú*

monsoon *jìfēng*

month *yuè*

monument *jìniànbēi*

moon *yuèliang*

mop *tuōbǎ*

more *gèngduō*

  more than *duōyú*

morning *zǎoshàng, shàngwǔ*

mosque *qīngzhēnsì*

mosquito net (on door) *shāmén*
  (on window) *shāchuāng*

mosquito *wénzi*

moth *é zi*

mother *māma, mǔqīn*

  my mother
    wǒde māma / mǔqīn

motor *mǎdá*

motorcycle *mótuōchē*

mountain *shān*

mountain climbing *dēngshān*

mouse (computer) *shǔbiāo*
  (animal) *lǎoshǔ*

mouth *zuǐ*

mouthwash *shùkǒuyè*

move *yídòng*

movie *diànyǐng*

movie theater *diànyǐngyuàn*

mozzarella *mòzéléilè*
  gānlào

Mr... *...xiānshēng*

Mrs... *... fūrén*

Ms... *...nǚshì*

much *duō*

  much better *hǎodeduō*

muffin *sōngbǐng*

mug *mǎkèbēi*

mumps *sāixiànyán*

muscles *jīròu*

museum *bówùguǎn*

mushrooms *mógu*

music *yīnyuè*

musician *yīnyuèjiā*

must: I must *bìxū: wǒ bìxū*

mustache *xiǎohúzi*

mustard *jièmo*

my... *wǒde...*

  my name is... *wǒjiào...*

N

nail *zhǐjiǎ*

nail clippers *zhǐjiǎdāo*

nail file *zhǐjiǎcuò*

nail varnish remover
xǐjiǎshuǐ

nail varnish
zhǐjiǎyóu

name *míngzì*

napkin *cānjīn*

narrow *zhǎi*

nation *mínzú*

national park
guójiā gōngyuán

natural *zìránde*

nausea *ěxīn*

navigate (v) *hángxíng*

near *jìn*

　is it near here?
　lí zhèlǐ jìn ma?

nearby *fùjìn*

necessary *bìyào*

neck *bózi*

neck brace *jǐngtuō*

necklace *xiàngliàn*

nectarine *yóutáo*

need: I need a...
　xūyào: wǒ xūyào...

needle *zhēn*

negative *dǐpiān*

Nepal *níbó'ěr*

nephew *zhízi*

Netherlands *hélán*

nettle *qiánmá*

network *wǎngluò*

neutral *língxiàn*

never *cóngláibù*

new *xīn*

newborn baby *xīnshēng'ér*

news *xīnwén*

newspaper *bàozhǐ*

New Year *xīnnián*

　Happy New Year!
　xīnniánhǎo!

New Zealand *xīnxīlán*

next *xià(yī)gè*

　next month *xiàgèyuè*

　next to... *zài... pángbiān*

　next week *xiàzhōu*

nice *hěnhǎo*

　how nice! *nà tàihǎole!*

niece *zhínǚ*

Nigeria *nírìlìyà*

night *yè*

nightclub *yèzǒnghuì*

nightgown *nǚshuìyī*

nightwear *shuìyī*

nine *jiǔ*

no *bú(shì)*

　no parking *jìnzhǐ tíngchē*

noisy *chǎonào*

nonstick *bùzhānguō*

noodles *miàntiáo*

noon: at noon *zhōngwǔ*

normal *zhèngcháng*

north *běi*

North and Central America
běiměizhōu

North Korea *cháoxiǎn*

North Sea *běihǎi*

Norway *nuówēi*

nose *bízi*

nosebleed *bíchūxiě*

nostril *bíkǒng*

not *bù*

　not for me *wǒbúyào*

notebook *bǐjìběn*

note pad *jìshìběn*
nothing *méishénme*
November *shíyīyuè*
now *xiànzài*
number (quantity) *shùzì*
  (numeral) *hàomǎ*
  telephone number
  diànhuà hàomǎ
nurse *hùshì*
nutmeg *ròudòukòu*
nuts *jiānguǒ*
nylon *nílóng*

O

o'clock *...diǎn*
oak *xiàngshù*
oar *jiǎng*
oats *yànmài*
occupations *zhíyè*
occupied *mánglù*
occupied (toilets) *yǒurén*
ocean *dàyáng*
October *shíyuè*
octopus *zhāng yú*
of *de*
  the name of the hotel
  lǚguǎn de míngzi
office *bàngōngshì*
office block *bàngōnglóu*
office equipment *bàngōngshèbèi*
office worker *bàgōng rényuán*
off-piste *xuědàowài*
often *jīngcháng*
oil (motor) *jīyóu*
  (vegetable) *zhíwùyóu*
ointment *ruǎngāo*
OK *hǎode, kěyǐ*
old (person) *lǎo*
  (things) *jiù*

olive oil *gǎnlǎnyóu*
olives *gǎnlǎn*
Oman *āmàn*
omelet *jiāndànbǐng*
on *zài*
  on the roof *zài fángdǐng*
  on the beach *zài hǎitān*
one *yī*
  that one *nàge*
onesie *yīng'ér liánjiǎokù*
one-way street *dānxíngdào*
one-way ticket *dānchéngpiào*
onion *yángcōng*
only *zhǐyǒu*
onto *zài ... shàng*
open (v) *kāi*
  (adj) *kāile*
opening times *kāimén shíjiān*
opera *gējù*
  Chinese opera *jīngjù*
opera house *gējùyuàn*
operating theatre
  shǒushùshì
operation *shǒushù*
operator (phone)
  (diànhuà)jiēxiànyuán
opponent *duìshǒu*
opposite *duìmiàn*
  opposite the...
  zài...duìmiàn
optometrist *yǎnjìngdiàn*
or *huòzhě*
orange (fruit) *chéngzi*
  (color) *chéngsè*
orange juice *chéngzizhī*
orchestra *yuèduì*
order (for goods, etc)
  dìnggòu, dìngdān
order (v) *diǎncài*

oregano *niúzhì*
organic *yǒujī(zāipéi)de*
other (ones) *qítā*
other: the other *lìngyīgè*
ounce *àngsī*
our(s) *wǒmende*
out *chūjú*
out: she's out *tābúzài*
outbuilding *fùshǔ jiànzhùwù*
outlet *chāzuò*
outside *wàimiàn*
oven mitt *kǎoxiāng shǒutào*
ovenproof *nàirè*
over: over there *zàinàli*
overalls *gōngzhuāngkù*
overdraft *tòuzhī*
overexposed
   bàoguāng guòdù
overhead bin
   tóudǐng suǒguì
overpass *lìjiāoqiáo*
owl *māotóuyīng*
own: on my own
   zìjǐ: wǒzìjǐ
oyster *háo*

P

Pacific Ocean *tàipíng yáng*
pack *zhǐhé*
pack of cards *yīfùpái*
package *bāoguǒ*
packet *bāo*
paddle *shuāngyèjiǎng*
paddy field *dàotián*
paediatrics *érkē*
page *yè*
pagoda *(bǎo)tǎ*
pail *shuǐtǒng*
pain *téng*

painting *huìhuà*
paints *yánliào*
pair *yīshuāng*
pajamas *shuìyī*
pak-choi *yóucài*
Pakistan *bājīsītǎn*
palette *tiáosèbǎn*
palm *shǒuzhǎng*
pan *chèngpán*
pan fried *jiānzhì*
pancakes *báojiānbǐng*
panda *xióngmāo*
pantihose *kùwà*
pants *kùzi*
papaya *fānmùguā*
paper *zhǐ*
paper clip *qūbiézhēn*
paper napkin *cānjīnzhǐ*
paprika *làjiāofěn*
Papua New Guinea *bābùyà*
   xīnjǐnèiyà
parachute *jiàngluòsǎn*
parachuting *tiàosǎn*
paragliding *huáxiángsǎn*
Paraguay *bālāguī*
parallel *píngxíng*
paramedic *jíjiù rényuán*
parasol *yángsǎn*
pardon? *qǐngzàishuōyībiàn?*
parents *fùmǔ*
park (n) *gōngyuán*
   (v) *tíngchē*
parka *huáxuěshān*
parking lot *tíngchēchǎng*
parking meter *tíngchējìshí*
   shōufèiqì
parking brake *shǒushāchē*
parking space *chēkù*
parmesan *pà'ěrmǎ gānlào*

parrot *yīngwǔ*
parsley *ōuqín*
parsnip *ōuzhōufángfēnggēn*
partner *pèi'ǒu*
party (celebration) *jùhuì*
　(group) *tuántǐ*
pass *chuánqiú*
pass (v) *chāochē*
pass (mountain) *guānkǒu*
passcode *mì mǎ*
passenger *chéngkè*
passport *hùzhào*
passport control
　hùzhào jiǎncháchù
password *mìmǎ*
pasta *yìdàlì miànshí*
pâté *ròujiàng*
path *xiǎolù*
patient (hospital, doctor, etc)
　bìngrén
patient *huànzhě*
pattern *zhǐyàng*
pause *zàntíng*
pavilion *tíngzi*
paving *shímiànlù*
pay *fùqián*
　can I pay, please? *wǒ kěyǐ*
　fùqián ma?
pay in (v) *cúnrù*
payment *fùkuǎn*
payphone *tóubìdiànhuà*
peach *táo*
peacock *kǒngquè*
peanut *huāshēng*
peanut butter *huāshēngjiàng*
pear *lí*
pecan *měizhōushānhétao*
pedal (v) *dēngtà*
pedal (n) *tàbǎn*

pedicure *zhǐjiǎ hùlǐ*
peel (v) *xiāopí*
pelvis *gǔpén*
penalty *fádiǎnqiú*
pencil *qiānbǐ*
pencil case *bǐdài*
pencil sharpener *zhuànbǐdāo*
pendant *xiàngliànzhuì*
penfriend *bǐyǒu*
penguin *qǐ'é*
penicillin *qīngméisù*
peninsula *bàndǎo*
penknife *xiǎodāo*
people *rén*
people carrier *liùzuò xiāngshìchē*
pepper (spice) *hújiāofěn*
　(red/green) *shìzijiāo*
peppercorn *hújiāolì*
pepperoni *yìdàlìlà xiāngcháng*
per
　...per cent *bǎifēnzhī...*
percentage *bǎifēnbǐ*
perfume *xiāngshuǐ*
perhaps *kěnéng*
perm *tàng(fà)*
perpendicular *chuízhí*
person *rén*
personal organizer *bèiwànglù*
personal trainer *sīrén jiàoliàn*
Peru *bìlǔ*
pesticide *shāchóngjì*
pet food *chǒngwù sìliào*
pet store *chǒngwùshāngdiàn*
pharmacy *yàofáng*
Philippines *fēilǜbīn*
phone *diànhuà*
phone card *diànhuàkǎ*
photo album *xiàngcè*
photo frame *xiàngkuàng*

photocopier *fùyìnjī*
photocopy *fùyìn*
photograph (n) *zhàopiàn*
    (v) *zhàoxiàng*
photographer *shèyǐngshī*
phrase book *chángyòngyǔ shǒucè*
physics (study) *wùlǐxué*
physiotherapy *lǐliáokē*
piano *gāngqín*
pickled *yānzì*
pickpocket *páshǒu*
pickup *shíyìnqì*
picnic *yěcān*
picnic bench *yěcān chángyǐ*
picture *túpiàn*
pie *xiànbǐng*
piece *piàn*
    a piece of... *yīpiàn...*
pier *zhànqiáo*
pig *zhū*
pigeon *gēzi*
pilates *pǔ lā tí*
pillar *dūn*
pillow *zhěntóu*
pills *yàopiàn*
pilot *fēixíngyuán*
pin *biézhēn*
pincushion *zhēndiàn*
pineapple *bōluó*
pink *fēnhóng*
pint *pǐntuō*
pip *zǐ*
pipe (smoking) *yāndǒu*
    (water) *guǎnzi*
pita bread *pítàbǐng*
pitch a tent (v) *zhī zhàngpéng*
pitch *luòqiúqū*
pitcher *tóu shǒu*

pizza *bǐsàbǐng*
place *dìfang*
place mat *cānjùdiàn*
place setting *cānjù bǎifàng*
plain *píngyuán*
plane (tool) *bàozi*
plane (air-) *fēijī*
planet *xíngxīng*
plant/s *zhíwù*
plant pot *huāpén*
plastic bag *sùliàodài*
plate *cāndié, pánzi*
plateau *gāoyuán*
platform *zhàntái*
platinum *bó*
play *xìjù*
play (in theater) *huàjù*
play (v)
    (sports, etc) *dǎ*
    (instrument) *tán,lā*
player *qiúyuán*
playground *yóulèchǎng*
playpen *yóuxì wéilán*
please *qǐng*
    please? *hǎoma?*
pleased *gāoxìng*
plug (electric) *chātóu*
plum *lǐzi*
plumber *guǎndàogōng*
plunger *chuāizi*
poach (v) *fèishuǐzhǔ*
pocket *yīdài*
point *diǎn*
poisoning *zhòngdú*
poisonous *yǒudúde*
poker *pūkèpái*
polaroid camera *bǎo lì lái xiàng jī*
police *jǐngchá*

police officer *jǐngguān*
police report *jǐngfāngbàogào*
police station *jǐngchájú*
polish *shàngguāngjì*
polite *yǒulǐmào*
politics *zhèngzhì*
polo *mǎqiú*
polyester *jùzhǐ*
pond *chítáng*
ponytail *mǎwěibiàn*
pool *yóuyǒngchí, shuǐchí*
poor (not rich) *qióng*
pop *liúxíng yīnyuè*
pop music *liúxíngyīnyuè*
popcorn *bàomǐhuā*
poppy *yīngsù*
poppy seeds *yīngsùzǐ*
porch *ménláng*
porch light *ménlángdēng*
pore *máokǒng*
pork *zhūròu*
porridge *màipiànzhōu*
port *gǎngkǒu*
porter *bānyùngōng, shǒuménrén*
portion *yìfèn*
portrait *rénxiàngzhào*
Portugal *pútáoyá*
possible *kěnéng*
post *yóujiàn*
post office *yóujú*
postage *yóuzī*
postcard *míngxìnpiàn*
poster *hǎibào*
pot plant *pénzāizhíwù*
potato *tǔdòu*
potato chips *shǔpiàn*
pottery *táoyì*
potty *yīng'ér biànpén*
pouch *yù'érdài*

poultry *qínròu*
pound *bàng*
pound (money) *yīngbàng*
pour (v) *zhùshuǐ*
powder *xiyǐfěn*
powdered milk *nǎifěn*
power *diànlì*
power cord *diànyuánxiàn*
power outage *tíngdiàn*
prawn *xiā*
pregnancy *huáiyùn*
pregnancy test *rènshēn jiǎnchá*
pregnant *huáiyùn*
present (gift) *lǐwù*
preservative *fángfǔjì*
press *xīnwénméitǐ*
press-up *fǔwòchēng*
pretty *piàoliang*
price *jiàgé*
price list *jiàmùbiǎo*
primer *dǐqī*
print *dǎyìn*
printer (machine) *dǎyìnjī*
prison *jiānyù*
private bathroom *zhuānyòng yùshì*
private jet *sīrén pēnqìshì fēijī*
private room *dānrén bìngfáng*
problem/s *wèntí*
produce stand *shūcàidiàn*
professor *jiàoshòu*
profits *lìrùn*
program *jiémù*
promenade *hǎibīn bùdào*
pronounce *fāyīn*
proud *zìháo*
prove (v) *fājiào*
province *shěng*
psychiatry *jīngshénkē*

public holiday *jiéjiàrì*
Puerto Rico *bōduōlígè*
puff pastry *nǎiyóupàofú*
pull *lā*
pulp *guǒròu*
pulse *màibó*
pumice (stone) *fúshí*
pump *qìtǒng*
pumpkin *nánguā*
pumpkin seed *nánguāzǐ*
punch (v) *chūquán*
purple *zǐsè*
push *tuī*
pyramid *léngzhuītǐ*

Q

quadriceps *sìtóujī*
quail *ānchún*
quarter *yīkè*
  quarter past one *yīdiǎnyīkè*
  quarter to two
  chàyīkèliǎngdiǎn
quay *mǎtóu*
question *wèntí*
queue (n) *duì*
quick *kuài*
quiet (place) *ānjìng*
quilt *miánbèi*
quince *yùnbó*
quinoa *kuínúyàlí*

R

rabbit *tù*
race *sàipǎo*
racecourse *sàimǎchǎng*
racehorse *sàimǎ*
racing bike *sàichē*
rack *jiàzi*
racket games *pāilèi yùndòng*

racket *qiúpāi*
racketball *duǎnpāibìqiú*
radiator *sànrèqì*
radio *shōuyīnjī*
radio station *guǎngbōdiàntái*
radish *xiǎohóngluóbo*
rail *tiěguǐ*
railcar *kèchēxiāng*
railroad *tiělù*
rain *yǔ*
  it's raining *xiàyǔle*
rain boots *chángtǒng*
  xiàngjiāoxuē
rainbow *cǎihóng*
raincoat *yǔyī*
rain forest *yǔlín*
raisin *pútáogān*
rake *pázi*
rally driving *qìchē lālìsài*
ramekin *gānlào dàngāomú*
rapeseed oil *càizǐyóu*
rapids *jīliú*
rarely *hěnshǎo*
rash (on body) *pízhěn*
raspberry *fùpénzǐ*
rat *lǎoshǔ*
rattle *bōlànggǔ*
raw *shēngde*
ray *hóngyú*
razor blades *tìxūdāopiàn*
razor *tìxūdāo*
read *dú*
reading (pastime) *dúshū*
reading light *yuèdúdēng*
ready meals *jíshíshípǐn*
ready *zhǔnbèihǎo*
real estate office
  fángdìchǎnshāng
rear light *wěidēng*

rear-view mirror *nèihòushìjìng*

receipt *fāpiào, shōujù*

receive (v) *jiēshōu*

reception (party) *zhāodàihuì* **(hotel, etc)** *jiēdàichù*

record *jìlù*

record (music) (n) *chàngpiān*

rectangle *chángfāngxíng*

recycling bin *lājī huíshōuxiāng*

red *hóng*

red meat *hóngròu*

red mullet *yángyú*

red currant *hóngcùlì*

reduced *jiǎnshǎode*

reduced-fat milk *bàntuōzhī niúnǎi*

reel in (v) *shōuxiàn*

reel *yúxiànlún*

reflexology *zúdǐ fǎnshè liáofǎ*

refrigerator *bīngxiāng*

reggae *léigài yīnyuè*

region *dìqū*

register *dēngjìbù*

relationships *rénjìguānxi*

relatives *qīnqi*

relaxation *fàngsōng*

release (v) *shìfàng*

religion *zōngjiào*

rent (for room, etc) *fángzū* **(v)** *zūyòng* **for rent** *chūzū*

repair *xiūlǐ*

report (n) *bàogào*

request (n) *qǐngqiú*

research *yánjiū*

reservation *yùdìng*

rest *xiūxi*

restaurant *cānguǎn*

result *jiéguǒ*

retired *tuìxiū*

return (v) (come back) *fǎnhuí* **(give back)** *huán*

return address *jìxìnrén dìzhǐ*

return date *guīhuánrìqī*

return ticket *wǎngfǎnpiào*

reverse (v) *dàochē*

rewind *dǎodài*

rhinoceros *xīniú*

rhubarb *dàihuáng*

rib *lèigǔ*

rib cage *xiōngkuò*

ribbon *duàndài*

rice (cooked) *mǐfàn* **(uncooked)** *mǐ*

rice bowl *fànwǎn*

rice cooker *diànfànbāo*

rice field *dàotián*

rice pudding *mǐfàn bùdīng*

ricecake *niángāo*

rich (person) *fù, yǒuqián*

riding boot *mǎxuē*

riding crop *mǎbiān*

riding hat *qíshǒumào*

right (not left) *yòu* **on the right** *zàiyòubiān* **(correct)** *duì*

rim *lúnquān*

rind *ròupí*

ring (on finger) *jièzhi*

ripe *chéngshúde*

river *héliú*

road *dàolù*

road bike *gōnglùchē*

road signs *jiāotōng biāozhì*

roadwork *dàolùshīgōng*

roast *kǎoròu*

roasted *kǎode*
robe *shuì páo*
rock climbing *pānyán*
rock concert *yáogǔn yīnyuèhuì*
rocks *yánshí*
Rocky Mountains *luòjī shānmài*
roller blind *juǎnlián*
roller coaster *guòshānchē*
rollerblading *lúnhuá*
rolling pin *gǎnmiànzhàng*
romance *àiqíngpiān*
Romania *luómǎníyà*
roof *wūdīng*
roof garden *wūdīng huāyuán*
roof tile *wǎpiàn*
roofrack *chēdīng xínglijià*
room (hotel, house) *fángjiān*
   (space) *kōng jiān*
room key *fángjiān yàoshi*
room number *fángjiānhào*
room service *kèfángfúwù*
root *gēn*
rope *shéngzi*
rose *pēntóu*
rosemary *mídiéxiāng*
rotten *làn*
rough *cūcāo*
round (adj) *yuánde*
router *lùyóuqì*
row *pái*
rowboat *huájiǎngchuán*
rubber (material) *xiàngjiāo*
rubber band *sōngjǐndài*
ruby *hóngbǎoshí*
rug *dìtǎn*
ruins *fèixū*
ruler *chǐzi*
rum *lǎngmǔjiǔ*
rump steak *niútuǐpái*

run *pǎo*
runner bean *hónghuācàidòu*
runway *pǎodào*
rush *cōngmáng*
rush hour *shàngxiàbān gāofēngqī*
Russia *éluósī*
rye bread *hēimiànbāo*

S

sad *shāngxīn*
saddle *chēzuò*
safe (not in danger) *píngān*
   (not dangerous) *ānqán*
safety goggles *hùmùjìng*
safety pin *ānquánbiézhēn*
saffron *zànghónghuā*
salad *shālā*
salami *sàlāmǐ xiāngcháng*
sales (company) *xiāoshòu*
sales clerk *shòuhuòyuán*
sales department *xiāoshòubù*
salmon *guīyú*
salt *yán*
salted *yánzìde*
same *yīyàng*
the same again, please
   zàiláiyīgè
sand *shā*
sandals *liángxié*
sandbox *shāxiāng*
sandcastle *shābǎo*
sandwich *sānmíngzhì*
sanitary napkins *wèishēngjīn*
sardine *shādīngyú*
Sardinia *sādīngdǎo*
satellite navigation (GPS)
   wèixīng dǎohángyí
satellite TV *wèixīngdiànshì*
Saturday *xīngqīliù*

sauce *jiàng*

sauces and condiments *tiáowèipǐn*

sauna *sāngnáyù*

sausage *xiāngcháng*

sauté (v) *chǎo*

savings account *chǔxù zhànghù*

savory *kāiwèide*

saxophone *sàkèsīguǎn*

say: how do you say...in Chinese *shuō :yòng hànyǔ zěnme shuō?*

scale *tǐzhòngjì*

scallion *xiǎocōng*

scallop *shànbèi*

scalp *tóupí*

scanner *sǎomiáoqì*

scared *jīngkǒng*

scarf *wéijīn*

school *xuéxiào*

science (study) *lǐkē*

scissors *jiǎndāo*

scoreboard *jìfēnpái*

scorpion *xiēzi*

Scotland *sūgélán*

scrambled eggs *chǎojīdàn*

screen *píngmù*

screw *luósīdīng*

screwdriver *luósīdāo*

scuba diving *shuǐfèi qiánshuǐ*

sea *hǎi*

sea bass *hǎilú*

sea bream *diāoyú*

seafood *hǎixiān*

search (v) *sōusuǒ*

seasonal *jì jié xìng*

seasons *jìjié*

seat *zuòwèi*

  take a seat *zuò*

seat belt *ānquándài*

second (in series) *dì'èr*

(of time) *miǎo*

second floor *èrcéng*

secretary *mìshū*

section (of store) *dìfāng*

security *ānquán*

security guard *bǎoān*

see *kànjiàn*

  I see! *shì zhèyàng!*

seedless *wúhé*

seesaw *qiāoqiāobǎn*

self-employed *gètǐhù*

sell *mài*

seminar *zuòtánhuì*

send (v) *fāsòng*

send off *jìchū*

senior citizen *lǎoniánrén*

sensitive *mǐngǎnxìngde*

sentence *pànxíng*

separately (pay) *fēnkāi(fù)*

September *jiǔyuè*

Serbia *sài'ěrwéiyà*

serious (illness) *yánzhòng*

serve *fāqiú*

server *fúwùyuán*

services *fúwù*

serving spoon *fēncānchí*

sesame oil *zhīmayóu*

sesame seed *zhīmazǐ*

set (theatre) *bùjǐng*

set honey *gùtǐfēngmì*

seven *qī*

sew (v) *féng*

sewing basket *zhēnxiànkuāng*

sewing machine *féngrènjī*

shallot *cōngtóu*

shallow end *qiǎnshuǐqū*

shampoo *xǐfàshuǐ*

shark *shāyú*

sharp *fēnglìde*
shave *guāhúzi*
shaving foam *tìxūpàomò*
she *tā*
shears *xiūlíjiǎn*
shed *péngwū*
sheep *yáng*
sheep's milk *miányángnǎi*
sheet (for bed) *chuángdān*
shell *ké*
shelves *gējià*
sherbet *guǒzhī bīnggāo*
sherry *xuělìjiǔ*
shin *xiǎotuǐ*
ship *chuán*
shirt *chènshān*
shock *xiūkè*
shoelaces *xiédài*
shoes *xiézi*
shoe store *xiédiàn*
shopping (activity) *gòuwù*
shopping bag *gòuwùdài*
shopping cart *gòuwùchē*
shopping mall *gòuwùzhōngxīn*
short *ǎi*
  (time) *duǎn*
shorts *duǎnkù*
shoulder *jiān*
shout (v) *jiàohǎn*
shovel *chǎn*
shower (in bathroom) *línyù*
shower curtain *línyù gélián*
shower gel *mùyùrǔ*
shower head *línyù pēntóu*
shrimp *xiā*
shut *guān*
shutter *kuàimén*
shy *xiūsè*
Siberia *xībólìyà*

siblings *xiōngdìjiěmèi*
Sicily *xīxīlǐdǎo*
sick *shēngbìng le*
side *miàn*
side effects *fùzuòyòng*
side order *pèicài*
side street *lùpángjiēdào*
sidewalk *rénxíngdào*
sieve *lùwǎng*
sight: the sights of... *fēngjǐng*
sightseeing *guānguāng*
sign *zhāopái*
signal *xìnhào*
signature *qiānmíng*
silk *sīchóu*
Silk Road *sīchóuzhīlù*
silt *xì shā*
silver *yín*
simmer (v) *wénhuǒ shāo,*
  wēi, dùn
sing *chànggē*
Singapore *xīnjiāpō*
singer *gēshǒu*
single bed *dānrénchuáng*
single room *dānrénjiān*
single: I'm single *dānshēn:*
  wǒshìdānshēn
sink (n) *shuǐchí*
sink (v) *xiàchén*
sinus *bí dòu*
siren *jǐngdí*
sirloin steak *niúshàngyāopái*
sister *zǐmèi*
sister (older) *jiějie*
  (younger) *mèimei*
sit *zuò*
sit-up *yǎngwòqǐzuò*
six *liù*
sixteen *shíliù*

skateboard *huábǎn*

sketch pad *sùmiáobù*

skewer *chuànròuqiān*

ski *huáxuěqiāo*

ski jacket *huá xuě fú*

ski slope *huáxuě pōdào*

skim milk *tuōzhī niúnǎi*

skin *pífū*

skin care *pífū hùlǐ*

skirt *qúnzi*

skis *huáxuěqiāo*

skull *lúgǔ*

sky *tiānkōng*

skydiving *tèjìtiàosǎn*

skyscraper *mótiān dàlóu*

slate *bǎnyán*

sledding *chéngqiāo huáxíng*

sleep *shuìjiào*

sleeper coach *yìngwòchēxiāng*

sleeping bag *shuìdài*

sleeping mat *shuìdiàn*

sleeping pill *ānmiányào*

sleeping *shuìmián*

sleet *yǔjiáxuě*

sleeve *xiùzi*

sleeveless *wúxiù*

sliced bread *qiēpiànmiànbāo*

sling *yīyòng diàodài*

slip *chènqún*

slip-on *wúdài biànxié*

slippers *tuōxié*

slope *shānpō*

slotted spoon *lòusháo*

Slovakia *sīluòfákè*

Slovenia *sīluòwénníyà*

slow down *jiǎnsù*

slow(ly) *màn*

SLR camera *dānjìngtóu*
   fǎnguāngzhàoxiàngjī

slug *kuòyú*

small *xiǎo*

smartphone *zhì néng shǒu jī*

smash *kòuqiú*

smell (have bad smell)
   nánwénde qìwèi

smile *wēixiào*

smoke (n) *yān*

do you smoke? *nǐ xīyān ma?*

smoke alarm *yānwù jǐngbàoqì*

smoked *xūnzhìde*

smoking *xīyān*

smoking area *jìnyānqū*

snack bar *língshí*

snacks *xiǎochī*

snake *shé*

sneeze *pēntì*

snooker *táiqiú*

snore (v) *dǎhān*

snorkel *shuǐxià hūxīguǎn*

snow *xuě*

snowboard *huáxuědānbǎn*

snowboarding *dānbǎn huáxuě*

snowmobile *jīdòng xuěqiāo*

so: so good *nàme: zhēnhǎo*
   not so much *búyào nàme duō*

soak (v) *jìnpào*

soap *féizào*

soap dish *féizàohé*

soccer *zúqiú*

soccer pitch *zúqiúchǎng*

socializing *shèjiāo*

socks *wàzi*

soda bread *sūdámiànbāo*

soda water *sūdá shuǐ*

sofa bed *shāfāchuáng*

sofa *shāfā*

soft (material, etc) *ruǎn*

soft drinks *ruǎn yǐnliào*

software *ruǎnjiàn*
soil *tǔrǎng*
soil (earth) *tǔ*
sole (of shoes) *xiédǐ*
somebody *yǒurén*
something *yǒuxiē dōngxi*
sometimes *yǒushí*
somewhere *mǒuchù*
son *érzi*
song *gē*
soon *mǎshàng*
sorry *duìbùqǐ*
  sorry? *nǐ shuō shénme?*
soufflé *dànnǎisū*
soundtrack *shēngdài*
soup *tāng*
soup bowl *tāngpén*
soup spoon *tāngchí*
sour *suān*
sour cream *suānnǎiyóu*
sourdough bread *suānmiànbāo*
south *nán*
South Africa *nánfēi*
South America *nánměizhōu*
South Korea *hánguó*
South Sudan *nán sū dān*
Southern Hemisphere *nánbànqiú*
souvenir *jìniànpǐn*
soy sauce *jiàngyóu*
soybeans *dàdòu*
Spain *xībānyá*
spark plug *huǒhuāsāi*
sparrow *máquè*
speak *jiǎng*
speaker *fā yán rén*
speaker stand *yīnxiāngjià*
specials *tèsècài*
spectators *guānzhòng*

speedboat *kuàitǐng*
spell (v) *pīnxiě*
spices *xiāngxīnliào*
spider *zhīzhū*
spin *xuánzhuǎn*
spin dryer *shuǎigānjī*
spinach *bōcài*
spine *jǐzhuī*
split ends *fàshāo fēnchà*
split peas *bànlìdòu*
spoke *fútiáo*
sponge cake *sōnggāo*
sponge *hǎimián*
spoon *sháozi*
sport *tǐyù*
sports *tǐyù yòngpǐn*
sports car *pǎo chē*
sports center *tǐyùzhōngxīn*
sportsman *yùndòngyuán*
spring (season) *chūntiān*
spring greens *nènyuánbáicài*
square *guǎngchǎng*
square foot *píngfāng yīngchǐ*
square meter *píngfāng mǐ*
squash (game) *bìqiú*
squat *dūnqí*
Sri Lanka *sīlǐlánkǎ*
St Lucia *shènglúxīyà*
stabilisers *wěndìnglún*
stable *mǎjiù*
stadium *tǐyùchǎng*
staff *yuángōng*
stage (theater) *wǔtái*
stainless steel *búxiùgāng*
staircase *lóutī*
stairs *lóutī*
stalls *zhèngtīng qiánpái zuòwèi*
stamp (for letter) *yóupiào*
stand *zhījià*

stapler *dìngshūjī*
staples *dìngshūdīng*
starfish *hǎixīng*
starfruit *yángtáo*
start (n) *kāishǐ*
starters *tóupán, kāiwèicài*
state *guójiā*
statement (e.g. witness) *zhèngcí*
statement (declaration) *chénshù*
station (railroad) *chēzhàn*
stationery *wénjù*
statue *diāoxiàng*
steak *niúpái*
steal: my bag has been stolen *tōu:wǒdebāo bèitōu le*
  what was stolen? *shénme bèitōu le?*
steamed *zhēng*
steering wheel *fāngxiàngpán*
stem *jīng*
stepdaughter *jìnǚ*
stepfather *jìfù*
stepladder *zhétī*
step machine *tàbùjī*
stepmother *jìmǔ*
steps *táijiē*
stepson *jìzǐ*
stereo *lìtǐshēng*
sterile *wújūn*
Sterling *yīngbàng*
Stew *dùncài*
stick *qiúgān*
sticky rice *nuòmǐ*
sting (injury) *zhēshāng*
stir (v) *jiǎodòng*
stir-fry *chǎocài*
stitches *fénghé*

stockings *chángtǒngwà*
stomach *dùzi, wèi (organ)*
stomach ache *wèitòng*
stone (gem) *bǎoshí*
stones *shítou*
stop (bus stop) *chēzhàn*
  stop! *tíng!*
  stop here *zài zhèlǐ tíng*
stopwatch *miǎobiǎo*
store *shāngdiàn*
store assistant *shòuhuòyuán*
  storm *bàofēngyǔ*
stove *lúzào*
straight; keep straight on *yīzhí, zhízǒu*
strap *jiāndài*
strapless *wújiāndài*
straw *xīguǎn*
strawberry *cǎoméi*
street *jiē*
street corner *jiējiǎo*
streetlight *lùdēng*
street sign *lùbiāo*
stress *yālì*
stretcher *dānjià*
string *xìshéng*
stroke *zhòngfēng*
stroller *zhédiéshì yīng'érchē*
student *xuéshēng*
student card *xuéshēngzhèng*
study *shūfáng*
stuffed *sāimǎnde*
stuffed animal *máoróngwánjù*
stupid *yúchǔn*
styles *jiànzhù fēnggé*
suburb *jiāoqū*
subway (underground) *dìtiě*
subway map *dìtiě xiànlùtú*
subway station *dìtiězhàn*

Sudan *sūdān*
sugar *táng*
suit (n) *xīzhuāng*
suitcase *xiāngzi*
sultana *wúhépútáogān*
summer *xiàtiān*
Summer Palace *yíhéyuán*
sun *tàiyáng*
sunbathe (v) *shài rìguāngyù*
sunbed *rìguāngyù yùchuáng*
sunblock (cream) *fángshàirǔ*
sunburn *shàishāng*
Sunday *xīngqītiān*
sundial *rìguǐ*
sunflower *xiàngrìkuí*
sunflower oil *kuíhuāzǐyóu*
sunflower seed *xiàngrìkuízǐ*
sunglasses *tàiyángjìng*
sunrise *rìchū*
sunroof *tiānchuāng*
sunset *rìluò*
sunshade *yángsǎn*
sunshine *yángguāng*
sunstroke *zhòngshǔ*
suntan lotion *fángshàiyóu*
supermarket *chāoshì*
support *zhīzuò*
suppository *shuānjì*
sure: I'm sure què dìng *quèdìng: wǒquèdìng*
 are you sure? *nǐ quèdìng ma?*
surf *lànghuā*
surfboard *chōnglàngbǎn*
surgeon *wàikē yīshēng*
surgery *zhěnliáoshì*
surprised *jīngyà*
suspect *xiányífàn*
suspension *qìchēxuánjià*
swallow *yànzi*

swan *tiān'é*
sweat (n) *hàn*
 (v) *chūhàn*
sweater *máoxiànshān*
sweatshirt *yùndòngshān*
swede *wújīnggānlán*
Sweden *ruìdiǎn*
sweep (v) *qīngsǎo*
sweet (adj) *tián*
 (confectionery) *táng*
sweet and sour *tángcù*
sweet potato *hóngshǔ*
sweltering: it's sweltering *mēnrè*
swim (v) *yóuyǒng*
swimming goggles *yóuyǒngjìng*
swimming pool *yóuyǒngchí*
swimming trunks *yóuyǒngkù*
swimming *yóuyǒng*
swimsuit *yǒngyī*
swing *qiūqiān*
Swiss chard *tiányècài*
switch *kāiguān*
Switzerland *ruìshì*
swivel chair *zhuànyǐ*
swordfish *jiànyú*
synagogue *yóutàijiào huìtáng*
synchronized swimming *huāyàng yóuyǒng*
Syria *xùlìyà*
syringe *zhùshèqì*
syrup (medicinal) *tángjiāng*
system *xìtǒng*

T

table *zhuōzi*
tablecloth *zhuōbù*
table tennis *pīngpāngqiú*

tablets *yàopiàn*
tack(v) *cūféng*
tackle *chǔlǐ*
Tai Chi *tàijíquán*
tailored *dìngzuòde*
Taiwan *táiwān*
take (transport) *chéng*
  (someone somewhere) *dài*
  (something somewhere) *dài*
take off (v) *qǐfēi*
take out (food) *wàimài*
talk (v) *shuōhuà*
tall *gāo*
tampons *miánsāi*
tan *zōnghèsè*
tandem *shuāngzuò zìxíngchē*
tank *guàn, xiāng*
Tanzania *tǎnsāngníyà*
Taoism *dàojiào*
tap water *zìlái shuǐ*
tape (cassette) *cídài*
  (adhesive) *tòumíngjiāodài*
tarragon *lónghāo*
tattoo *wénshēn*
tax *shuì*
taxi *chūzūchē*
taxi driver *chūzūchē sījī*
taxi stand *chūzūchēzhàn*
tea *chá*
  tea with milk *nǎichá*
teabag *chábāo*
teacher *lǎoshī*
team *qiúduì*
teapot *cháhú*
tear *yǎnlèi*
teddy bear *tàidíxióng*
teenager *qīngshàonián*
telegram *diànbào*

telephone *diànhuà*
  telephone card *diànhuàkǎ*
  telephone number *diànhuàhàomǎ*
telescope *tiānwén wàngyuǎnjìng*
television *diànshìjī*
television series *diànshì liánxùjù*
tell *gàosù*
temperature (weather) *qìwēn*
temple *sìmiào*
ten *shí*
tenant *fángkè*
tendon *jiàn*
tennis *wǎngqiú*
tennis racket *wǎngqiúpāi*
tent *zhàngpéng*
tent pole *zhàngpénggān*
tequila *lóngshélánjiǔ*
terminal (airport) *hòujīlóu*
terrace café *lùtiān kāfēizuò*
terraced *liánpáishì*
terracotta Army *bīngmǎyǒng*
terrible *zāogāo*
test *jiǎnchá*
test (hospital) *huàyàn*
text (SMS) *wénzì xùnxī*
textbook *jiàokēshū*
Thailand *tàiguó*
than *bǐ...*
  smaller than *bǐ...xiǎo*
thank you *xièxienǐ*
that: that woman *nèigè nǚde*
  that man *nèigè nánde*
  what's that? *nà shì shénme?*
theater *jùyuàn*
their(s) *tāmende*
them *tāmen*
then (after that) *ránhòu*
  (at that time) *dàoshí*

therapist *zhìliáoshī*
there *nàlǐ*
  there is/are *yǒu...*
  is/are there...? *yǒu...ma?*
  there isn't/aren't... *méiyǒu...*
thermals *bǎonuǎn nèiyī*
thermometer *tǐwēnjì*
thermos flask *rèshuǐpíng*
thermostat *zìdòng tiáowēn qì*
these *zhèxiē*
they *tāmen*
thick *hòu*
thief *xiǎotōu*
thigh *dàtuǐ*
thin (thing) *báo*
  (person) *shòu*
thing *dōngxi*
think *xiǎng*
third floor *sāncéng*
thirsty: I'm thirsty *wǒ kǒukě*
thirty *sānshí*
this: this street *zhè tiáo jiē*
  this is... *zhèshì ...*
  what's this? *zhèshì shénme?*
those *nàxiē*
thousand *qiān*
  ten thousand *wàn*
thread *xiàn*
three *sān*
thriller *jīngxiǎnpiān*
throat *hóulóng*
throat lozenge *rùnhóupiàn*
through *jīngguò*
throw *rēng*
thumb *mǔzhǐ*
thunder *léi*
thunderstorm *léiyǔ*
Thursday *xīngqīsì*
thyme *bǎilǐxiāng*

thyroid gland *jiǎzhuàngxiàn*
Tibet *xīzàng*
ticket *piào*
  admission ticket *ménpiào*
  airline ticket *jīpiào*
  train/bus ticket *chēpiào*
ticket gates *jiǎnpiàokǒu*
ticket inspector *jiǎnpiàoyuán*
ticket office *shòupiàochù*
tie (around neck) *lǐngdài*
tiger *hǔ*
tile *cízhuān*
time *shíjiān*
  next time *xiàcì*
  on time *zhǔndiǎn*
  what time is it? *xiànzài jǐdiǎnle?*
timer *jìshíqì*
timetable *shíkèbiǎo*
tip (money) *xiǎofèi*
tire (car) *chētāi*
tired *lèi*
tissue(s) *zhǐjīn*
to *dào*
  to England *qù yīnggélán*
toad *chánchú*
toast (bread) *kǎo miànbāopiàn*
toasted sandwich *kǎosānmíngzhì*
toaster *kǎomiànbāojī*
tobacco *yāncǎo*
today *jīntiān*
toddler *yòu'ér*
toe *jiǎozhǐ*
toenail *zhǐjiǎ*
toffee *tàifēitáng*
tofu *dòufu*
tofu shop *dòufudiàn*
together *yīqǐ*
toilet *cèsuǒ*

toilet brush *mătŏngshuā*
toilet paper *wèishēngzhĭ*
toilet seat *mătŏngzuò*
toiletries *huàzhuāng yòngpĭn*
toll booth *shōufèizhàn*
tomato *xīhóngshì*
tomorrow *míngtiān*
ton *dūn*
toner *shuǎngfūshuĭ*
tongue *shé*
tonic (water) *kuíníngshuĭ*
tonight *jīntiānwǎnshàng*
too (also) *yě*
   (excessively) *tài*
toolbox *gōngjùxiāng*
tools *gōngjù*
tooth *yáchĭ*
toothache *yátòng*
toothbrush *yáshuā*
toothpaste *yágāo*
topaz *huángyù*
topping *zhuāngshìpèiliào*
tornado *lóngjuǎnfēng*
tortoise *guī*
tour (n) *lǚxíng*
tour bus *guānguāngbāshì*
tourist *yóukè*
tourist attraction
   yóulǎn shèngdì
tourist bus *yóulǎnchē*
tourist information *lǚyóu*
   wènxúnchù
tourist information office
   lǚyóu fúwùzhōngxīn
towards *xiàng...fāngxiàng*
towel *máojīn*
towel rail *máojīnjià*
town *chéngzhèn*
town hall *shìzhèngtīng*

track *guǐdào*
track and field *tiánjìng yùndòng*
tracksuit *yùndòngfú*
traditional *chuántŏng*
traffic *jiāotōng*
traffic lights *jiāotōng*
   xìnhàodēng, hónglǜdēng
trailer *tuōchē*
train *lièchē, huŏchē*
train station *huŏchēzhàn*
tram *yŏuguǐdiànchē*
transformer *biànyāqì*
translate *fānyì*
transplant (v) *yízhí*
transportation *jiāotōng yùnshū*
trash *lājī*
trash can *lājītŏng*
travel agent *lǚxíngshè*
traveling *lǚyóu*
travel-sickness pills
   yùnchēyào
tray *tuōpán*
tray-table *gēbǎn*
treadmill *pǎobùjī*
tree *shù*
trekking *chángtú lǚxíng*
tremor *zhèndòng*
triangle *sānjiǎo*
triceps *sāntóujī*
trifle *rǔzhīsōnggāo*
trim (v) *xiūjiǎn*
trimmer *cǎo píng xiū jiǎn jī*
Trinidad and Tobago *tèlìnídá hé*
   duōbāgē
trip (journey) *lǚxíng*
tripod *sānjiǎojià*
trombone *chánghào*
tropical fruit *rèdàishuǐguŏ*
tropics *rèdài*

trough *sìliàocáo*
trout *zūnyú*
trowel *níchǎn*
truck *zàizhòngqìchē*
true *zhēnde*
truffle *kuàijūn*
trumpet *xiǎohào*
trunk (of car) *qìchē xínglixiāng*
trunks *yǒngkù*
T-shirt *T xù shān*
try (test) *shìyàn*
try *chángshì*
tub *yùpén*
Tuba *dàhào*
Tube *ruǎnguǎn*
Tuesday *xīngqī'èr*
tulip *yùjīnxiāng*
tumble dryer *gǔntǒngshì hōnggānjī*
tumbler *píngdǐbōlibēi*
tuna *jīnqiāngyú*
Tunisia *tūnísī*
turkey *huǒjī*
Turkey *tǔ'ěrqí*
turmeric *jiānghuánggēn*
turn (v) *zhuǎn*
    turn left *zuǒzhuǎn*
    turn right *yòuzhuǎn*
turnip *luóbo, wújīng*
turn signal *zhuǎnxiàngdēng*
turpentine *sōngjiéyóu*
turret *jiǎolóu*
turtle *hǎiguī*
tweezers *nièzi*
twelve *shí'èr*
twenty *èrshí*
twenty-one *èrshíyī*
twig *xìzhī*

twin-bedded room *shuāngchuángjiān*
twins *shuāngbāotāi*
two *èr, liǎng*

U

ugly *chǒu*
ultrasound *chāoshēngbō*
umbrella *yǔsǎn*
uncle *shūshu*
unconscious *bùxǐng rénshì*
under *zài...xiàmian*
underpass *dìxiàtōngdào*
undershirt *bèixīn*
understand: I don't understand *míngbai: wǒ bù míngbai*
underwear *nèiyīkù*
unfortunately *yíhànde(shì)*
uniform *zhìfú*
United Arab Emirates *ālābó liánhé qiúzhǎngguó*
United Kingdom *yīngguó*
United States *měiguó*
university *dàxué*
university lecturer *dàxuéjiǎngshī*
unpasteurized *wèi jīngguò bāshìxiāodúde*
unsalted *wúyánde*
upset *shēng qì*
urgent *jǐnjí*
utility room *zá wù jiān*

V

v-neck *V xínglǐng*
vacation *jiàqī*
    on vacation *dùjià*
vaccination *yùfángjiēzhǒng*
vacuum cleaner *xīchénqì*

valley *shāngǔ*
valve *fámén*
vanilla *xiāngcǎo*
varnish *qīngqī*
vase *huāpíng*
veal *xiǎoniúròu*
vegetables *shūcài*
vegetable oil *zhíwùyóu*
vegetarian *sùshí*
veggie burger *shūcài hànbǎo*
vein *jìngmài*
venetian blind
  bǎiyèchuāng
Venezuela *wěinèiruìlā*
venison *yěwèiròu*
vent *tōngfēngkǒng*
very *hěn, fēicháng*
very well (OK) *hěnhǎo*
vest *mǎjiǎ*
veterinarian *shòuyī*
video game *diànzǐyóuxì*
video tape *lùxiàngdài*
Vietnam *yuènán*
view (scenery) *jǐngsè*
village *cūnzhuāng*
vine *pútáoshù*
vinegar *cù*
vintage (car) *lǎoshìqìchē*
viola *zhōngtíqín*
violin *xiǎotíqín*
virus *bìngdú*
visa *qiānzhèng*
vise *hǔqián*
vision *shìlì*
visit (place) *cānguān*
  (people) *bàifǎng*
visiting hours
  tànwàngshíjiān
visor *tóukuīmiànzhào*

vitamins *wéishēngsù*
vodka *fútèjiājiǔ*
voice *shēngyīn*
voicemail *yǔyīnxìnxiāng*
voice message
  yǔyīn xùnxī
volcano *huǒshān*
voltage *diànyā*
volume *tǐjī*
vomit (v) *ǒutù*

W

wading pool *értóng xìshuǐchí*
waffles *huáfūbǐng*
wake up (v) *xǐnglái*
waist *yāo*
waistband *yāodài*
wait *děng*
waiting room (clinic)
  hòuzhěnshì
waitress *nǚfúwùyuán*
Wales *wēi'ěrshì*
wall *qiáng*
  the Great Wall of China
  chángchéng
wall light *bìdēng*
wallpaper *bìzhǐ*
walk (go by foot) *zǒulù*
walk (go for a walk) *sànbù*
walnut *hétao*
walrus *hǎixiàng*
want: I want *yào: wǒ yào*
ward (hospital) *bìngfáng*
warehouse *cāngkù*
warm *nuǎnhuo*
warm up (v) *rèshēn*
wash (v) *xǐ*
washbasin *xǐshǒuchí*

washer *diàn piàn*
washer-dryer *xǐyī gānyījī*
washing machine *xǐyījī*
washing powder *xǐyīfěn*
washing-up liquid *xǐjiéjīng*
wasp *huángfēng*
wastebasket *fèizhǐlǒu*
waste disposal *lājīchǔlǐ*
watch (wrist) *shǒubiǎo*
   (v) *kàn*
water *shuǐ*
water bottle *shuǐpíng*
watercolor paint *shuǐcǎihuà yánliào*
watercress *dòubàncài*
waterfall *pùbù*
water heater *guōlú*
watering can *pēnhú*
watermelon *xīguā*
water polo *shuǐqiú*
waterskier *huáshuǐzhě*
waterskiing *huáshuǐ*
watersports *shuǐshàng yùndòng*
water valve *zhǐshuǐshuān*
water wings *chōngqìbìquān*
wave *bōlàng*
wax *là*
we *wǒmen*
weak *xūruò*
weather *tiānqì*
website *wǎngzhàn*
wedding *hūnlǐ*
wedding cake *hūnlǐ dàngāo*
wedding dress *jiéhūn lǐfú*
wedding reception *hūnyàn*
wedge (shoes) *pō gēn xié*
Wednesday *xīngqīsān*
weedkiller *chúcǎojì*
weeds *zácǎo*

week *xīngqī*
weigh (v) *chēng zhòngliàng*
weight (for scales) *fámǎ*
weight training *zhòngliàng xùnliàn*
welcome *huānyíng*
   you're welcome *búkèqì*
well: I don't feel well
   wǒ gǎnjué bùshūfu
west *xī*
Western (n) *xībùpiān*
Western-style *xīshì*
wet *shī*
wetsuit *qiánshuǐfú*
wet wipe *shīzhǐjīn*
whale *jīng*
what? *shénme?*
wheat *xiǎomài*
wheel *lúnzi*
   (vehicle) *chēlún*
wheelbarrow *dúlún shǒutuīchē*
wheelchair *lúnyǐ*
when? *shénme shíhòu?*
where? *nǎr,nǎlǐ*
where: where is...?
   ...zài nǎlǐ?
which: which one? *nǎ(yī)gè?*
whiplash *tóujǐngbù sǔnshāng*
whipped cream *guànnǎiyóu*
whiskers *sāixū*
whiskey *wēishìjì*
white *bái*
white bread *báimiànbāo*
white chocolate *báiqiǎokèlì*
white meat *báiròu*
white rice *báimǐ*
white spirit (chemical) *xīshìjì*
who? *shéi?*
   who's calling? *nínshìnǎwèi?*

whole *wánzhěng*
wholegrain *quángǔwù*
whole milk *chúnniúnǎi*
whole-wheat bread *hēimiànbāo*
why? *wèishénme?*
wide *kuān*
width *kuān*
wife *qīzi*
Wi-Fi *wú xiàn wǎng luò*
win (v) *yíng*
wind *fēng*
windbreak *fángfēngpíng*
window *chuānghù*
windpipe *qìguǎn*
windsheild *fēngdǎng*
windsheild wiper
  yǔshuā
windsurf board *fānbǎn*
wine *pútáojiǔ*
  wine glass *jiǔbēi*
  wine list *jiǔdān*
wing mirror *hòushìjìng*
wings *chìbǎng*
winner *yíngjiā*
winter *dōngtiān*
winter sports
  dōngjì yùndòng
wipe (v) *cāshì*
wire wool *gāngsīróng*
with *hé*
withdrawal slip
  qǔkuǎndān
without *méiyǒu*
witness *zhèngrén*
wok *chǎocàiguō*
wolf *láng*
woman *nǚrén, nǚshì*
women's clothing
  nǚzhuāng

women's toilets *nǚcèsuǒ*
womenswear *nǚzhuāng*
wood *mùtou*
wooden spoon *mùsháo*
wood glue *mùcáijiāo*
wood stain *mùcái rǎnsèjì*
wool *yángmáo*
word *cí*
work (n/v) *gōngzuò*
  it's not working *huàile*
workbench *gōngzuòtái*
workshop *gōngzuòjiān*
world map *shìjiè dìtú*
worm *chóngzi*
worried *yōulù*
worry: don't worry
  dānxīn: biédānxīn
worse *gèngchà*
wound *shāngkǒu*
wrap *juǎn*
wrapping *bāozhuāng*
wrapping paper
  bāozhuāngzhǐ
wrench *bānshǒu*
wrinkle *zhòuwén*
wrist *shǒuwàn*
wristband(s) *hùwàn*
write (v) *xiě*
  could you write it down?
  nǐ néng xiěxiàlái ma?
wrong *cuò*

X

X-ray *X guāng*

Y

yacht *yóutǐng*
Yangtze Gorges *chángjiāngsānxiá*
Yangtze River *chángjiāng*

yard *mǎ*
yawn (v) *dǎhāqian*
year *nián*
yeast *jiàomǔ*
yellow *huáng*
Yellow River *huánghé*
Yellow Sea *huánghǎi*
yes *shì(de)*
yesterday *zuótiān*
yet: not yet *hái: háiméi*
yogurt *suānnǎi*
yolk *dànhuáng*
you *nǐ*
   (formal) *nín*
   (plural) *nǐmen*
young *niánqīng*
your(s) *nǐde*
   (plural) *nǐmende*

Z

zebra *bānmǎ*
zero *líng*
zest *wàipí*
zipper *lāliàn*
zone *dìyù*
zoo *dòngwùyuán*
zoom lens
   biànjiāo jìngtóu

ACKNOWLEDGMENTS

ORIGINAL EDITION

Senior Editors Simon Tuite, Angela Wilkes
Editorial Assistant Megan Jones
US Editor Margaret Parrish
Senior Art Editor Vicky Short
Art Editor Mandy Earey
Production Editor Phil Sergeant
Production Controller Inderjit Bhullar
Managing Editor Julie Oughton
Managing Art Editor Louise Dick
Art Director Bryn Walls
Associate Publisher Liz Wheeler
Publisher Jonathan Metcalf

**Produced for Dorling Kindersley by:
SP Creative Design**
Editor Heather Thomas
**Language content for Dorling
Kindersley by:
g-and-w publishing**
Translator Shuang Zou
Editor Cheng Ma
Typesetting g-and-w publishing

Dorling Kindersley would like to thank the following for their help in the preparation of this book: Shuang Zou, Cheng Ma, Isha Sharma, Janashree Singha, Nishtha Kapil, and Neha Ruth Samuel for editorial assistance; Doug Hewitt and Meenal Goel for design assistance; Rose Horridge in the DK Picture Library; Sandra He and Paula Regan for help with photographic material.

PICTURE CREDITS

The publisher would like to thank the following for their kind permission to reproduce their photographs:
(Key: a-above; b-below/bottom; c-centre; l-left; r-right; t-top)
Alamy Images: David Crausby 112cla; Eye Ubiquitous 117cla; Mike Goldwater 35crb; Belinda Lawley 84bl; Martin Lee 54tr; Photo Agency EYE 58crb; PhotoSpin, Inc 40crb; David Robinson/Snap2000 Images 36bl; Ulana Switucha 34; **Alamy Stock Photo:** Sean Pavone 4; Stanca Sanda 19 clb; **Corbis:** Wu Hong/ epa 22; Studio Eye 64cla, 65br; **Courtesy of Renault:** 28–29t; **Getty Images:** Asia Images Group 94br; C Squared Studios 64cl; Alex Cao 117 cra; Reggie Casagrande 148; Datacraft 141t; Foodcollection 54clb, 58br (chicken feet); Imagemore Co., Ltd 94br, 117clb; Alex Mares-Manton 53br; Travel Ink 97clb; ULTRA.F 18clb; **iStockphoto.com:** Alvin Teo 65bl; **Photolibrary:** Asiapix 140; **PunchStock:** Moodboard 8; **123RF.com:** Brad Wynnyk 18 crb; Cobalt 108 cr; Norman Kin Hang Chan / Bedo 109 clb; Cobalt 134 bl; Cobalt 156 br

All other images © **Dorling Kindersley**
For further information, see: **www.dkimages.com**

NUMBERS

0 零 *líng*	**6** 六 *liù*	**12** 十二 *shí èr*	**18** 十八 *shí bā*	**40** 四十 *sìshí*	**90** 九十 *jiǔshí*
1 一 *yī*	**7** 七 *qī*	**13** 十三 *shí sān*	**19** 十九 *shí jiǔ*	**50** 五十 *wǔshí*	**100** 一百 *yībǎi*
2 二 *èr*	**8** 八 *bā*	**14** 十四 *shí sì*	**20** 二十 *èrshí*	**60** 六十 *liùshí*	**101** 一百零一 *yībǎi líng yī*
3 三 *sān*	**9** 九 *jiǔ*	**15** 十五 *shí wǔ*	**21** 二十一 *èrshí yī*	**70** 七十 *qīshí*	**500** 五百 *wǔbǎi*
4 四 *sì*	**10** 十 *shí*	**16** 十六 *shí liù*	**22** 二十二 *èrshí èr*	**80** 八十 *bāshí*	**1,000** 一千 *yīqiān*
5 五 *wǔ*	**11** 十一 *shí yī*	**17** 十七 *shí qī*	**30** 三十 *sānshí*	**81** 八十一 *bāshí yī*	**10,000** 一万 *yīwàn*

ORDINAL NUMBERS

first 第一 *dìyī*	**fourth** 第四 *dìsì*	**seventh** 第七 *dìqī*	**tenth** 第十 *dìshí*
second 第二 *dìèr*	**fifth** 第五 *dìwǔ*	**eighth** 第八 *dìbā*	**twentieth** 第二十 *dìèrshí*
third 第三 *dìsān*	**sixth** 第六 *dìliù*	**ninth** 第九 *dìjiǔ*	**fiftieth** 第五十 *dìwǔshí*